S0-ADF-164

Life After ...
Art and Design

Thousands of students graduate from university each year. The lucky few have the rest of their lives mapped out in perfect detail – but for most, things are not nearly so simple. Armed with your hard-earned degree, the possibilities and career paths lying before you are limitless, and the number of choices you suddenly have to make can seem bewildering.

Life After ... Art and Design has been written specifically to help students currently studying, or who have recently graduated, make informed choices about their future lives. It will be a source of invaluable advice and wisdom to graduates of creative subjects (whether you wish to use your degree directly or not), covering such topics as:

- Identifying a career path that interests you – from advertising to interior design
- Seeking out an opportunity that matches your skills and aspirations
- Staying motivated and pursuing your goals
- Networking and self-promotion
- Making the transition from scholar to worker
- Putting the skills you developed at university to use in life.

The *Life After ...* series of books are more than simple 'career guides'. They are unique in taking a holistic approach to career advice – recognising the increasing view that, although a successful working life is vitally important, other factors can be just as essential to happiness and fulfilment. They are the indispensible handbooks for students considering their future direction in life.

Sally Longson is a life coach and well-known writer and media commentator in the field of careers.

ENTERED JUL 1 9 2007

Also available from Sally Longson

Life After ... Business and Administrative Studies
0-415-37591-6

Life After ... Engineering and Built Environment
0-415-37592-4

Life After ... Language and Literature
0-415-37593-2

Life After ...
Art and Design

COLUMBIA COLLEGE LIBRARY
600 S. MICHIGAN AVENUE
CHICAGO, IL 60605

A practical guide to life after your degree

Sally Longson

Routledge
Taylor & Francis Group

LONDON AND NEW YORK

First published 2006
by Routledge
2 Park Square, Milton Park, Abingdon, Oxon OX14 4RN

Simultaneously published in the USA and Canada
by Routledge
270 Madison Ave, New York, NY 10016

Routledge is an imprint of the Taylor & Francis Group, an informa business

© 2006 Sally Longson

Typeset in Sabon by
HWA Text and Data Management, Tunbridge Wells
Printed and bound in Great Britain by
TJ International Ltd, Padstow, Cornwall

All rights reserved. No part of this book may be reprinted or repro-
duced or utilised in any form or by any electronic, mechanical, or
other means, now known or hereafter invented, including photocopy-
ing and recording, or in any information storage or retrieval system,
without permission in writing from the publishers.

British Library Cataloguing in Publication Data
A catalogue record for this book is available from the British Library

Library of Congress Cataloging-in-Publication Data
Longson, Sally
    Life after – art and design: a practical guide to life after your degree/
    Sally Longson. – 1st ed.
        p.   cm.
    Includes bibliographical references and index.
    1. Art – Vocational guidance. 2. College graduates – Vocational
    guidance.
    I. Title: Practical guide to life after your degree. II. Title
    N8350.L66 2006
    702.3´73–dc22   2005036629

ISBN10: 0–415–37590–8
ISBN10: 0–203–08842–5
ISBN13: 978–0–415–37590–0

Contents

Preface

You've graduated or you're coming to the end of your degree, and now you're contemplating your next steps.

Here's some good news, you have one of the most sought after skills employers want – creativity and innovation. Employers want people who can come up with new ideas, take risks and think laterally. If you can combine those skills and talent with commercial awareness and an understanding of the importance of the bottom line, strong self-presentation and networking skills, then you have an exciting future ahead of you. Creativity can have a huge impact on business performance.

The United Nations estimates that globally the creative and cultural industries are growing at a rate of 10 per cent per annum. In some countries, they are growing at a rate of 5–20 per cent a year. People have more time and money to spend on products and services produced by the creative and cultural industries, such as film, the arts, culture, and digital entertainment. Advertisers and designers are core in creating a 'must have that' desire in customers for products and services they might not otherwise have wanted. For most of us, having the product or experience in our lives says something about who we are. It sends out a message to those we meet and know, and attracts new people to us, and gives us that 'feel good' buzz.

Many artists and designers enjoy a career of a patchwork of short-term contracts and projects, self-employment and freelancing, work outside their profession and low monetary rewards. Life is particularly difficult for newcomers and you will need to be particularly resilient and very focused if you want to make a career out of what you love doing. But your university experience has given you tremendous self-assurance, plus self-belief. You know you can take the initiative and plan your life, and you are probably more alert than most to change and the opportunities it presents.

There is a lot of support and know-how available for people who want to set up on their own. Of all graduates, those from creative arts courses are most likely to do so in areas such as craft, music and fine art. They may not make much money from it, but they love what they do and are often the envy of those in other jobs who've always wanted to be a painter, sculptor, interior designer, fashion designer, etc.

Having a degree does not guarantee having a good job. *Nothing* in life guarantees you a job. And the term 'graduate job' has taken on different connotations as it covers a far greater range of roles and careers than it used to. Many graduates now expect three years to pass before they secure the permanent professional posts they seek or, in many cases, move into self-employment. That intervening time may be spent doing lower level work in administration, retail, leisure and tourism, food and drink, the financial and business services sector, taking roles as temps, sales assistants, pub and bar work and call centres. Alternatively, many will take a 'bread and butter' job in the day while working at what they consider to be their 'real' job when they get home at night, in the hope that in the future, the latter may become so successful they can give up the day job. Keep your career and life goals and ambitions at the forefront of your mind and really strive to achieve them. Your creative capabilities should help you come up with an idea or a solution to really kick-start your career, and open your mind to new possibilities and adventures.

As you identify any change you want to make in life, there are two key stages to the process. First, raise your own awareness of the change or decisions which need to be made. Second, take personal responsibility for making that change happen and implementing those decisions until you get the desired result. Rather than living life in a maze of today, imagine yourself looking at your own life from a helicopter in flight. It's much easier to see the way forward when you're looking at the big picture from a distance, so keep the wide screen view at the forefront of your mind and tackle the detail in chunks.

This book talks holistically about *life* after a degree, and not just your career. Careers are only part of life – there are a whole host of other things which are also important, such as relationships, finance and lifestyle. The main emphasis will be on career and work, however, because they affect many other areas of life. It will take you through the what, why, where, who, when and how of life, so that you can really get specific about what you want and how you're going to make it happen. It is an overview of life after your degree. Life is very much what you make of it – it's not a dress rehearsal. The more energy and effort you put in, the more you'll get out of it. Let's get started!

Chapter 1

Decisions, decisions ...

What happens now? What happens next?

What happens from now on depends on how determined you are to bring your hopes and aspirations, dreams and ambitions to fruition and the timescale within which you want to do it. Your future plans may be very clear to you, or you may be kicking lots of ideas about, or just not have a clue. What you *do* know is that there are lots of decisions to make and plans to be laid – but what, exactly? Where do you start?

Looking at the next few months

If you've already left university, you may have happily spent the summer enjoying a break at home before considering what happens next. The start of the academic year may feel strange as you realise that for the first time, perhaps in your life, you do not have to go back to school, college or university. You're free to do as you like. This may also be strange to the people you live with, such as your parents. They may not be used to you being around and may start giving you odd jobs to do which interfere with your day and which you may resent. Meal times may be punctuated with discussions about your future and when you're going to get a 'real' job and visitors to the house ask you about your plans. It may feel as though life is going backwards fast, instead of moving on to greater things. Build a structure into your life, even if you have no work or study to go to. Keeping to a routine now will help you when you start work.

You may have studied part time for your degree while holding down a full-time job, working two or three hours a night and trying the patience of family members as you disappear to study yet again. You've probably pleaded with the boss for more time off, spent lunch times doing research on the Internet and sneaked the odd sickie to get that assignment done. And now you're faced with many free hours and you feel a bit lost. It's nice to have a rest from all that study, but having risen to one challenge, you want another. If you're still at university, create time *now* to plan your career. This involves participating in activities such as constructive work experience, internships, developing your portfolio and web of industry contacts, voluntary work, attending careers and trade events and research into the job market, finding out what resources are available if you want to become self-employed, considering further study, visiting the careers service in person and online and analysing your own strengths and capabilities. Allocate even three hours a week out of 168 during your degree, and you will be well on the road to securing your immediate future. You'll also have time to fill any missing gaps in your CV to strengthen any future job or course applications and make deadlines. If you are a post-graduate student, this equally applies. Visit your careers service to see how they can help you, and don't leave it too late.

Start building bridges from where you are now to where you want to be. The more foundations you can lay down now, the easier life will be later.

Take control. Get organised

Create a folder – call it something like 'Life After University' – and put everything you need to work on in it. It will save you time searching for pieces of paper and information. If you've got a PC or lap top, create a life and career folder on that, too, for emails and bookmark useful websites you visit regularly. In addition, plan for the presentation and expansion of your portfolio, ideas, references, scribbles, doodles, articles you've cut out or printed off, and notes of conversations you've had with fellow students, artists, designers, industry contacts, employers and tutors and anyone else you talk to. Consider the following:

- ◆ How are you going to organise your portfolio?
- ◆ Where will you continue your arts, craft and design after you've left university – what space will you need and can you

negotiate for it, for example, if you're moving back home with your parent(s)?

* What facilities and equipment will you need? Where will you find those? What can you set up on your own where you live? Can you tap into facilities in the area?
* If you plan to work for someone else, how much activity of an artistic or design nature do you think you will do outside of the working day for your own enjoyment?

Efficient organisation will clear your mind of clutter and enable you to work more effectively. Both collections – your 'life after' folder and your portfolio – should grow week by week as you add to them and expand your knowledge, contacts and ideas and work.

Then look ahead

There are several key decisions to make about your life after graduating. These vary from the urgent and/or important, to those things which simply need to be dealt with, such as *'What will I do with all my books and materials?'* and *'Which friends do I want to keep in touch with?'* The latter two questions need to be cleared from your mind, to prevent them from muddying your thinking, so that you can focus on the all-important bigger picture.

There will be urgent decisions you need to make today. The important ones are not usually time pressured but they affect the Big Picture, i.e. your life. An important and urgent decision may be: do you accept that offer of a post-graduate place you had yesterday? It's Tuesday now, you've got until Thursday at 5 p.m. to decide.

Two major issues which you will almost certainly want to deal with are those of career and finance. Devote more time and energy on these now and you'll reap the rewards in the long term. Socialising may be fun but it won't bring you the best rate of return career-wise, nor will it help you pay off your debts. Building clarity around your future career and life goals will help you to work towards them. Plotting your career and working your way up the ladder will bring a higher salary, or making progress with your own business will, for example, help you sort out your finances and debts.

Let's follow these two areas in life further.

Do career and financial audits

Table 1.1 demonstrates questions to ponder in such audits. Doing an exercise like this empowers you because you're choosing to address the situation. You're looking at it head on, dealing with known facts rather than assumptions or guesses. You can move forward by creating an action plan and implementing it. With regard to debts, it is better to know what your bottom line is to prevent yourself getting any further into debt. You may have a student debt of £15,000, but how much further are you prepared to allow yourself to build that up before you start paying it back? £20,000? £30,000? It doesn't mean you'll never go for a wild night out with your friends again but it could mean that you look for other ways to have a wild time so that you can control your finances more tightly. Do it jointly with friends in the same boat and work together to deal with it. There are times when we don't like the decisions we have to make; they are uncomfortable and don't fit in well with the lifestyle we want.

Table 1.1

Career	Finance
What do I want to achieve in life?	How much do I owe?
What is important to me?	Who do I owe it to?
What do have I to offer the world?	How much interest am I paying each
What am I going to do next?	lender monthly?
What could I learn to ensure I get to where I want to be?	What could I do to reduce this interest?
What are my ambitions and aspirations, dreams and hopes?	What incomings do I have now?
	What am I spending it on?
How far do I want a career which uses the knowledge I've acquired of my subject?	What do I have left?
	What could I do to cut back on my spending?
Could I go on to further study?	How could I pay back my loans and
Do I need a break?	debts?
Where in the world do I want to work?	Who could help me?
	What could I do to get the best deal on
How far shall I go in my career?	everything?
Where can I get constructive, informed advice (e.g. university careers service, Prospects)?	What could I do to supplement my income?
	When will I start paying everything
Who do I need to support me?	back?
What action(s) will I take to move me closer to where I want to be?	Where can I get constructive, informed advice (e.g. bank, building society, student loan company)?
	What action(s) will I take to achieve my financial and life goals?

But discipline never did anyone any harm and can frequently bring unexpected rewards, not least of which is self-respect and an in-built self-belief that you can turn an uncomfortable situation around.

Take action now!

1 List the decisions you need to make now and in the next six months.
2 What have you done so far towards making these decisions?
3 What else do you need to do or to know in order to decide? How will you get that information and where will you get it from?
4 Whose help will you need?
5 When do you need to make each decision?
6 What action will you take?

Many of the decisions in one area of our life will impact on others. For instance, your career choice will affect where you live and work, the structure of your life and the people you work with and/or socialise with. It will impact on your standard of living and your overall happiness. You may need to undertake further training, learning and development to acquire your professional status. Career choice can determine the hours you work and whether you're on call or not, the pace of your working day and your stress levels. The effort you put into your career will affect your ability to pay back your loans and start laying strong financial foundations to your life.

Are you an effective decision maker?

You can learn a lot about yourself from the way you've made past decisions. Take two decisions you've made about your university life or course. Ask yourself:

1 What motivated you to take these decisions?
2 *How* did you make them? For example, was it by gut instinct, by careful research and thought, weighing up the pros and cons, tossing a coin, following the lead of others, force of circumstance or meeting the expectations of others? What process did you follow?

3   Who influenced your decisions and subsequent actions? Who could you have involved more or less?
4   What, if anything, held you back from making decisions and how did you overcome it?
5   Is a pattern emerging about your decision making? What does it tell you about the way you make decisions? Are there patterns which aren't helping you that you need to break?
6   How can you make your decision making more effective?

In making any decision, there are various factors to take into account as shown in Table 1.2.

Decision-making skills transfer well in life, from making career choices to buying a home. Such skills are essential at work, whether you are self-employed, an employee or the boss, in making business decisions such as the clients you choose to work with, which suppliers you choose to work with and whether you should relocate

Table 1.2

Possible factors influencing your decision	Choosing modules to study	Choosing your career
Your strengths and skills	What you're naturally good at and wanted to build your skills in	Same for career
Your interests	Following your passions	Same for career – this is what you want to do
What was available?	The modules on offer at your university	What is on offer in the region you work in?
Personal fit	You had a lot of time and respect for the tutor and got on well together; you thought he'd bring out the best in you	You like where the company is going and what it stands for; you met the guys and felt comfortable with them
Long-term plans	You want to go into marketing so this fitted well with your career plans	You choose an employer who can meet your aspirations
How you make decisions	for example '… Ran out of time – just ticked the box for something to do' 'Gut feeling. Everything felt right about this'	for example '…Went for the first thing I saw – can always change later' 'The moment I walked into the place, I knew it was right for me'

your business to a more cost-effective area. Action plans to implement our decisions are often interrupted when unexpected obstacles
make the journey more of a roller-coaster ride, but a focus on the
end result will help steer us through the rougher patches.

Focus on the result you want and the obstacles will shrink

Often when faced with a decision, we tend to focus too much on
possible problems and the negative. *'There are too many graduates...'*, *'not enough time in the day...'*, *'I don't want to...'*. Problems have a way of shrinking when put into the context of what we
really want. Let's say you get the offer of a dream career from an
employer you'd love to work for. The only hitch is that you don't
know anyone in the town you'd be living in. It's a totally new area
to you. *'Where will I live if I go somewhere new?'* you may ask.
But compared to the job offer, which you're wild with excitement
about, the accommodation problem is minor. You know you'll sort
it somehow. You could lodge for a while as you look. Your new colleagues may know about housing opportunities and good inexpensive places to live. There will be local papers, the HR department
may be able to help you or your new boss. You may have friends in
the area from university. The most important thing is that you've
got the offer you wanted. You found somewhere to live and made
new friends at university; you can do it again.

---

*Have faith in your own ability to create a life for yourself even if you
move to a place where you don't know anyone.*

Yes, it's hard, but you've done it before and survived. You've handled
such problems before and you can do so again, thanks to those transferable skills you developed at university, such as the abilities to:

1   start completely afresh – new people, new place, new things to
    learn, new challenges;
2   take part in and contribute to an organisation – previously,
    your university, now the workplace, the community, new
    friends;
3   find your way around and learn the ropes;
4   ask the right questions of the right people to get the answers
    you need;

5   network and get to know people across the organisation – as
     you did at university;
6   take the initiative and make things happen – a day at univer-
     sity or college which – lectures and tutorials apart – was pretty
     much your own;
7   show how adaptable and flexible you are in juggling work,
     study and social activities, often changing plans at the last
     minute;
8   organise your time;
9   hunt out new friends and like-minded people you can particu-
     larly relate to;
10   relate to people of all different sorts of backgrounds, nation-
     alities and abilities.

University has taught you to think, to question, to be creative, to
think laterally, to challenge, to research, to find solutions to problems and to interact. Those skills will never be wasted. And the
more you stretch yourself and expand them, the more powerful a
resource they will become.

Wait a minute ...

Before you start making decisions, consider what's really important
to you.

Where are you going? How does the decision fit into the bigger
picture?

A key starting point to making successful decisions involves
knowing what is right for you in life or work. You need a strong
sense of self-worth and self-awareness. These things encompass areas such as the roles you want to play in life, your career interests,
ambitions, aspirations, the environments and conditions you thrive
in and learn best in, the things you need around you to make you
happy and feel fulfilled and those things that are important to you
and what you couldn't do without, i.e. your values. Know what you
want, and life has more purpose. You'll move faster because you
don't deviate from your route spending time doing things you don't
want to do. Many people simply wait for that lucky break to knock
on their door. Unfortunately, they have a long wait. You can create
your own luck, as Dr Wiseman points out in his excellent book *The
Luck Factor* (see Further Reading at the end of this book).

What's important to you?

When you live by your values, you look forward to the start of a new day or week, and you wake up with a happy heart. Life feels right, you feel fulfilled with a strong sense of your own self-worth. Your goals, hopes and aspirations seem easier to strive for because you're at your best as you work towards them. You know you're making the right choices and decisions and moving in the right direction. Similarly, the company which recruits staff with values equal to its own has a good feel about it. The staff are happy, motivated, fulfilled and feel appreciated. They look forward to going to work and are a tight-knit team.

Five signs when life – and work in particular – does not encapsulate your values are:

1 You can't perform properly. You get very tired trying to work at something that doesn't gel with you while pretending that all is well.
2 You're frustrated and short tempered, especially as a new working week looms.
3 It's lonely. Everyone else seems to be on a different wavelength to you.
4 You keep thinking, *There must be more to life than this!* This thought persists over time, making you increasingly frustrated and more angry.
5 You're disappointed in yourself because you know that you should cut your losses and leave, but you can't find the *courage* to do it.

Of course, you may find the perfect match and then something hinders its progression: a technological innovation, a change in the markets, a drop in demand, restructuring, redundancy. Employers understand that it takes time to find the right match, and when reading your CV, they consider your achievements, progression, development, future career plans and the person who lies behind the words on paper and portfolio. But it's your responsibility to find the right career and role.

Table 1.3 gives examples of life and career values. Which ones are important to you to have or be in your life and career to make you truly happy and feel successful?

Having considered which values are important to you, you can build a life and career which incorporates them. For example, if achievement is very important to you, you could look for careers where results are exceedingly important and measured, such as sales roles.

Select the top eight values which are essential to you from those you've ticked and create a picture of what they mean to you – don't make any assumptions about them. Get the foundations right. If you think that things such as travel, holidays and a good social life are your values, consider what those things *give you* or *provide you with* and you'll have your real values. Then rank those eight in order. Which one is most important? Which values could you *not* do without? And which are you *not* prepared to compromise on?

Compromising in life will bring more win–wins

At some stage in life, you'll need to compromise. For example, let's say you want to work for an ethical company, but the only position you were offered in six months was from a company which, in your eyes, was unethical, what would you do? Would you refuse to take the job and uphold your values or take the offer up and move on as soon as you could?

Table 1.3

Winner	Participant	Contributor
Continuous change	Change where needed	Little change
Security	Stability	Risk
Creativity	Performer	Conformity
Compassion	Fair	Faith
Achiever	Influencer	Supporter
Recognition	Status in community	Appreciated
Success	Work–life balance	Fulfilment
Autonomy	Independence	Managed
Visionary	Implement	Support
Adventure	Spirituality	Pleasure
Driver, creator	Follow the leader	Win–win
Wealth	Rewarded	Feel-good factor
Happiness	Freedom	Other

What happens now?

Figure 1.1 gives you questions to ponder and answer.

Many graduates have no clear idea of what they want to do after university, so they take whatever comes their way in the first three to five years after graduation, as shown in Figure 1.2.

This runway to career take-off may be longer and tougher in terms of getting that lucky break, the opportunity or gap in the market, especially as you are probably trying to begin a new life at the same time. You may hook a lower-level job, just to get going, and you'll need a real rocket thrust of persistent effort to get yourself to where you aspire to be. Keep focused on your goal, and you'll head in the right direction. If you lose that focus, your ambitions will take longer to achieve, or they may lose their impetus and fizzle out.

Do you want a job, a career or a business?

These are very different things. Jobs fit well into short-term plans and bring the money in, but they don't necessarily stretch you or

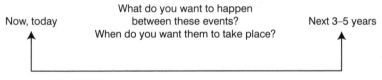

| Now, today | What do you want to happen between these events? When do you want them to take place? | Next 3–5 years |

- Set up my own business and be making a living from my craft
- Working freelance as a …
- Settled down into life after university
- Working in animation
- Qualified as a …
- Paid off …% of my student loans and started to …
- Found my partner for life
- Got professional qualifications as a …

Figure 1.1

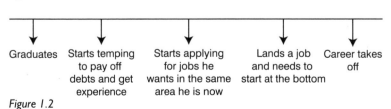

Graduates | Starts temping to pay off debts and get experience | Starts applying for jobs he wants in the same area he is now | Lands a job and needs to start at the bottom | Career takes off

Figure 1.2

pay well. Consequently they can make you feel bored and disillusioned, especially when you weigh up your salary against your student debts. Careers may run over a course of time, enabling you to develop your skills, expertise and experience in one particular sector, often climbing the career ladder to reach the upper echelons of the business and sector. You may have a view of the top of this ladder from the bottom or you may create the view, rung by rung, as you climb up. Of course, a job can become a career if you take the initiative, yank it up a gear and get yourself noticed, i.e. take two rungs at once. You could also decide to set up your own business, which enables *you* to make all the decisions: what you will sell, the who, what, when, why, how and where.

By the end of your life, you may have had all of these.

How does your career fit into your life?

You need to find the work–life balance that's right for you, your life and your dependants. At first, this may be hindered as you devote time to establishing yourself and getting a foot on the work and housing ladders, putting bricks and blocks down to get the life you want – the house, family life, network of friends, security, professional qualifications where appropriate, the opportunity for advancement and professional growth, recognition and appreciation. You may prefer to focus on having fun, rather than sorting out your career and life. *Well, there's always next year.*

A hunger for success at work can seriously impact on our quality of life. If your goal was to make your first million within three years after leaving university, and you succeeded, but you lost all your friends in the process because you were always working, would you still deem that a success? Some graduate programmes demand that you dedicate 60, 70, 80 or even 90 per cent of your life to work. You may be prepared to give that early in your career if it takes you to where you really want to be, or you may prefer to opt for a more sensible work–life balance which takes you to a rung on the ladder which you're happy with.

What matters is the *degree of control* we each have over our work–life balance. If you decide to work 100 hours a week to make that first million, that's your choice. Work–life balance becomes an issue when we feel we *don't* have a choice; that other people are making decisions for us about the hours we need to put in. Some employers place a higher priority on work–life balance than others.

The most demanding employer may be the person who runs their own business.

As you create a vision of your future career, build specifics into the picture so that you can build plans around them. For example:

* What is your career goal, outcome or end result? If it makes things easier, look at this over a three to five-year period.
* Why is this important to you?
* How exactly is your career important to you?
* Where do you want to be doing it?
* When are your timescales/deadlines for achieving your goal?
* Who will you be doing it with?
* Who can help you?
* How will you get there? What are the different ways you could reach the outcome you want?
* What can you do to boost your chances of success?
* What can you control? What is outside your control?
* Which deadlines do you need to look out for, such as applying for post-graduate courses, work experience placements and internships?
* What in life and in your career are you *not* prepared to risk, e.g. your integrity, values, standards, expectations of yourself, key relationships ... and what *are* you prepared to risk?

The *why* is important. If you don't understand *why* something is important to you, it is far less likely to happen. If you understand how a goal relates to your values – for example, keeping fit is important to you because you value good health which gives you the freedom to live your life to the full – then you're more likely to achieve it.

Wherever you are, pinpoint careers help available to you

Find out what careers advisory services are available to you where you are *now*, face-to-face, online and by telephone. Sometimes you just need to sit down and talk through your future with someone whom you can trust who is impartial, qualified and trained. Tap into local universities and colleges, your old university and other private agencies in your area for access to careers information and support. Most higher education institutions allow graduates to use their facilities for up to two or three years after graduation and they may also help graduates from any university wishing to move into, remain in or return to their area. You may be charged for some services.

Finally, don't forget that your degree has taught you many transferable skills. Use the forward and strategic planning skills you acquired throughout your degree experience to plan your career and life. Take the initiative. Put your brain to work.

Summary action points

Look back at your life overall:

1   How much has it consisted of what you want so far? What efforts have you put in to make sure that happened?
2   What lessons have your past choices taught you as you look to your future?
3   What do you want to achieve *in your life* in the next five years? What would that mean to you?

Chapter 2

Creating your career

Building on your creative and innovative spirit

This chapter is all about helping you to create a vision of what you want your career to consist of. Even if you already have a picture, use the self-assessment exercises to add depth to it. Stand back and look at yourself from that helicopter viewpoint, and the distance will help you think more clearly.

Many arts and design students enter careers which are relevant to their own studies, and they have the highest take up of self-employment among all graduates, moving into the creative industries. The sector is defined by the UK's Department of Culture, Media and Sport as 'Those industries which have their origin in individual creativity, skill and talent and which have a potential for wealth and job creation through the generation and exploitation of intellectual property'. Collectively, they cover:

- advertising
- architecture
- arts and antiques market
- crafts
- design
- digital/new media
- fashion
- film, video, TV and radio
- marketing
- music
- performing arts
- photography
- publishing
- computer games

These industries are growing rapidly, partly because people have more time and access to money to spend on the products and services the sector produces. They have more of a 'desire to have' in the luxury good items and want to stock their homes with the best of everything and they're prepared to pay for it. When customers buy a product, they are often telling us something about their lifestyle, values and beliefs. A product design tells us a lot. The companies those services and products come from may be huge or very small outfits. They all contribute to what is a fast growing economy and one on which most governments are seeking to capitalise, since they are selling statements, ideas, values and concepts. Many governments view the arts and crafts industries as a way to regenerate less well off economic areas and/or to send the message about their culture abroad, through creating arts and crafts which portray their country's history. This means that there may be initiatives to assist you, the graduate. This could either help you on the way to setting up your own business or joining a micro-business (under five people) or small business (under 50 people).

You may have specialised on one or two areas within your degree or, indeed, focused entirely on the subject for the duration. Rather than canter laboriously through one career after another in the art and design world, this chapter will pose various questions for you to consider when plotting your life after graduation, so that you can highlight what is important to you.

Do you want to take up a career directly related to your career studies?

This could mean either:

1   working with art and crafts, probably for yourself or a very small company; or
2   working in the design industry (with small and medium-sized firms, or as a freelancer).

Either of these options will enable you to use the skills and knowledge you have every day at work. But it's important to bear in mind that business knowledge will be essential to succeed. You could turn your hand to arts and crafts, setting up your own business or outsource your services and skills out as a freelance. Either way, you will still need to tackle the subjects of pricing and fixing the price of an item or service for sale at such a price that it will appeal to customers yet cover your overheads and make you a profit. You'll need business and entrepreneurial skills to start up, promote and market your services and products, meet customer demand and handle all the various business functions demanded of the small business owner.

What will life be like working for a small company or being the boss of one?

In the art and design world, many companies are of the medium, small and micro-business size. They may take longer to root out and undoubtedly the allied industries working to support them will be able to help you locate them, but they have a lot to offer. Small companies have many advantages: you'll probably enjoy more varied responsibilities and see the entire design or artistic process from start to finish, being involved at every stage. You'll have a finger on the pulse and know what's happening and you'll need to be resilient and pro-active in developing your career and seeking the training you need. The work environment will be less structured and hierarchical, and the decision-making processes faster.

There is, of course, a flip side, either to running your own business or working for a small company. Put yourself in the shoes of the company owners as *business* people. They've probably put a huge amount of time and money into their company, yet they still go through peaks and troughs of work. One week they will be working flat out, while the next they will be gloomily wondering where the next piece of business will come from. They will need more staff for peak busy periods and very few in others and that need can change from one hour to the next. The bosses probably spend too much time and energy and focus on the 'doing,' rather than devoting it to strategic planning and business development. Many bosses are being strangled by legislation such as health and safety and employment laws. Every time he or she takes on a new employee, they worry whether the new member of staff will disappear on maternity or paternity leave or indeed fit in with the rest of the team. Will there be sufficient work long term to justify another member of staff? Visit any of the small business networking sites and you'll quickly get a feel for the issues concerning them. They will prepare you for what lies ahead and the working culture you may find.

Aside from thinking about what sort of business you would like to join or create, stand back and look at the trends taking place worldwide and how those are impacting on how people are employed, for example, on a freelance, contract or permanent basis. Increasing employment regulations *could*, for example, benefit the freelance. Could you market your skills on a freelance basis, setting up a pricing structure for your services and invoicing clients for your work?

How far do you want to specialise?

In any sector, there are specialist areas. You may have focused on them already as part of your degree. Is there one or several parts of your degree course which you wish to develop into a career? Can you see yourself doing that day in and out and making a living out of it, or would you prefer to transfer some of the skills and knowledge you have acquired to allied industries?

Figure 2.1 shows examples of these specialist areas.

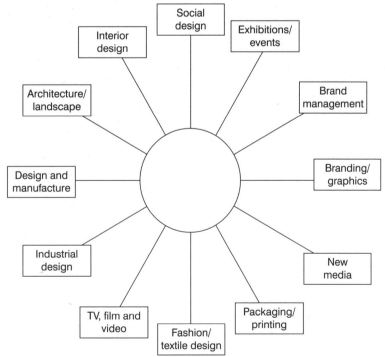

Figure 2.1

These specialist areas again break down into different categories and focus. Interior designers may focus on individual customers, designing bathrooms or kitchens or re-makes, or they may work for other businesses, such as the hotel sector, office planning, schools or hospitals. They will need to take their customers' and clients' business values and vision to heart if they are to come up with the right design for their products and services.

What sort of customers or clients do you want to provide a product or service for?

◆ Business/organisation to business/organisation, perhaps creating a new design for a company's offices or designing an exhibition.

◆ Business to customer, in which case you're selling your company's goods to a customer – such as art supplies to an individual buying art materials.

◆ Customer to customer, for example, becoming a wedding photographer or making jewellery on commission from individuals.

◆ Public sector or voluntary organisations, or international bodies.

This opens you up to the possibility of working at your craft in a huge range of specialist companies, such as interior design offices, architects, building suppliers, the public sector, shop fitters, furniture designers, retail shop furnishing departments, fabric, furnishing and furniture suppliers, shop fitters, research and development departments, animation studios, special effects departments, computer games industry, exhibition and display designers, advertising agencies, public relations firms, desk top publishing companies, printing companies, packaging firms, publishers, newspapers, magazine companies, museums, web designers, colouring companies, importers and exporters, education, wholesalers, clothing companies, textile manufacturing companies and being self-employed. Many of these will provide products or services to their customers or clients and be working to their specification and trying to incorporate their brand and values in the end product. This is where art, design, creativity and business intertwine very strongly.

How far do you believe your career as a designer or artist will incorporate other essential skills?

The answer may surprise you. You may think that you simply want to design or make a product or craft, that business is nothing to do with you, that's the realm of business people in sober suits and the occasional flashy tie. But whether you work for someone else or set up alone, you'll need to use business and transferable skills.

When people buy a product or engage in a service, they want it to look and feel good. Designers play a key role in working with businesses to help them capture the imagination of potential customers and clients, to create a desire for a particular product – such as a really flash sports car – and an experience which makes them feel good. The touch, smell, feel and sight and sound of a product can have a profound effect on the user, not just on initial sight and experience, but every time the user lays eyes on it. Designers can create the feel-good factor between a company and its clients, connecting them by producing a product or service which inspires, motivates, pleases and thrills. That same connection can in itself ensure that the customer comes back for more and that he recommends the service or product to everyone he knows.

Look around at a workplace. How much thought has gone into its design, to make people feel welcome, make it easier for them to work and get motivated? You use colour, light, texture, culture, values, space and tone and play on the environment to achieve the maximum effect. A designer will need to spend some time thinking about what the business is trying to achieve so that he can then go out to create the right effect. The end product is talking to the customer and telling them a story about the company, about life and about themselves.

In short, designers need key transferable skills such as empathy, the ability to communicate and listen, to solve their problems, to engage everyone in the process who will be using the end result, and then present effectively their ideas. They need to understand their client's brand, values, vision and goals through careful questioning, listening, challenging and analysing. Then they need to produce something which will make the product stand out, but for some considerable time and not just for the moment, within the allocated budget and timescale. Planning, organising, discussing, researching, identifying – they are all essential skills which artists and designers need.

Are you creating for your pleasure – or that of your client?

There is a difference in creating for yourself and for a client. As an artist, for example, do you want to provide a bespoke service to a client, or a range of products from which the client can choose? You may be commissioned to make a glass structure for a client to a specification. You will need to meet with that client to discuss their requirements, price the project, including the materials required (which you will need to source, perhaps approaching several producers so that you know you're getting the best deal which doesn't necessarily mean the cheapest). The time it will take you to do the work should include the number of meetings and calls you will have with your client. You'll need to work to your client's deadlines, not your own, perhaps to coincide with a product the company will be launching. As designer, you'll need to sell the concept(s) you come up with to your client, answer questions they have and then take the project through to completion. You may even need to talk to the local, regional and national press about it, so you'll need to represent your company and profession well.

There will be times when your client is expecting one thing and you know that it is not right or possible, perhaps for reasons of health and safety, design or engineering feat or the materials you'll be working with or the budget you'll be working to. Some clients constantly change their minds about what they want. From start to completion, just as you need to manage an idea from conception to fruition, you need to manage your client, too, being honest and open about good and bad news, and keeping in touch with how their project is progressing. There'll be a budget to work to, and you'll need to find the right materials and equipment to both please the client and their purse. You'll also need to work with teams to ensure that deadlines are met. As a manager, you may be in charge of your design team to control the entire process and make sure that the right people are brought in at the right stage in proceedings.

Are you ready for your clients' and the public's displeasure with your work?

Your innovations and designs need to be pleasing not just to the client but sometimes to the general public too. One of the hard parts about being an architect, for example, is discovering that not everyone likes your creation. It is on display for all to see, externally at least, and subject to public scrutiny. You need a thick skin to take on board comments, both positive and negative about 'your' creation, and to handle discontent. You need to have the self-confidence to handle feedback that you may not agree with or like. This is also the case when you first show your creations to your clients.

How do you want to express your creativity?

You can express your creativity in a number of ways, such as hands-on as a potter or painter would; or by other means, such as the person transferring the creativity talents they have within themselves and applying them to industry, commerce, etc. in terms of thinking up solutions to problems.

- ◆ Hands on
  Potter, glassmaker
- ◆ By passing your knowledge and skills onto others
  Teaching
  Art therapy
  Lecturer
- ◆ Art and design is useful
  Arts administration
  Art gallery management
  Advertising
  Retail buying
- ◆ Design based
  Graphic design
  Interior design
- ◆ New ideas and concepts
  Social enterprise
- ◆ Applying creativity to industry
  Workshops
  Web localiser
  Solving problems by creating solutions
- ◆ Concepts/ideas
  Environmental concepts
  Sustainability design

Areas such as these above may, in large part, involve you working freelance or for small companies – hopefully your own. They will demand a certain amount of entrepreneurial vision, implementation of that vision as a manager and hands-on technical art and design, as you've been taught.

Do you want to use your knowledge and skills to complement your actual role?

There are a number of careers in which your art and design knowledge will be very useful, but not form the core of what you do, such as advising art investors, art administration, arts suppliers, working in galleries, bringing exhibitions together and working for affiliated bodies such as the Design Council, Crafts Council, relevant magazines and press and websites. Your degree knowledge will enhance your effectiveness on the job, or an employer may simply look for someone 'with a strong interest in art/contemporary art/culture'. An employer would probably pick a graduate with a degree in Museum Studies because they would have have a fair amount of knowledge and skill which could be relevant to his company in the future.

Theatres, studios, community programmes, festivals, educational specialists, galleries, orchestras, publishers, councils and museums will all need marketing, finance, HR, organisers and planners, so even if you develop these specialist niches elsewhere first, you can always transfer to work for them later. A strong understanding of the business world could help when it comes to, for example, corporate sponsorship and entertainment. Your studies are very useful, perhaps as an art teacher, art therapist or working in a field such as art administration or an activities organiser in a residential home.

You may also be able to work by passing your knowledge on to people, either through the compulsory schooling age with young people, adult education, further and higher education, tutoring on painting holidays, or even working as an art therapist. You could also coach people on how to make money from their businesses and skills.

What are your passions and motivators?

If you want to be happy and successful in your career, envisage what your best possible day at work would look like and what you would get for your trouble. Get passionate. Find something to do which really inspires and motivates you and stirs you to action, which gives you a *real* buzz. If you have a real passion for developing people, you could go into training or teaching, but use your creative talents and skills to bring out the best in people. If you love buying and selling, your creativity will help in deciding how to promote products and ranges and coming up with ideas to make your company stand out. This is all about your vocation and reason for working. Consider the following questions.

+ What excites and inspires you?
+ What are you passionate about?
+ What do you want to make a difference to or particularly do something about?
+ How do you want to make a difference to the world, a local community or a group of people?
+ What secret dreams and aspirations do you have?
+ What makes you jump out of bed in the morning?
+ How could you make money from your dream?

How hungry are you to turn these passions into action?

You may have some passions and interests, causes and aspirations in mind already. How hungry are you to pursue them in your career? Are you ravenous to take them on board, or just wanting to nibble at them a bit and take on other bites as well? How fulfilled would you be if you turned them into a career which you worked at 48 weeks of the year and thought about outside working hours? Without that hunger, that ravenous feeling, you're not likely to follow them through and succeed. If you nibble a bit here and snack on something there, you'll feel less fulfilled, and still feel a longing for something which will really hit the spot.

How far do you want to make a living from the skills and knowledge you've acquired on your degree course?

Assess how far you see yourself making a living from the skills and knowledge you have acquired on your degree course.

1   I want my income to come totally from them – I want to design and make furniture/design websites/paint sports cars.

2   I want my income to come partly from them and partly through a more stable line of work such as teaching adults or supply teaching. The teaching will keep the money coming in, but I'll have enough time and energy to get my business off the ground.

3   I want to combine them with something which enables me to run my own business but use the creativity I have.

4   I expect to have a career in something else for the time being – I'll get a full-time job in administration while building up my portfolio and getting ready for a career as a full time artist/photographer/designer.

5   I am happy to work for someone else such as a potter, photographer, designer, etc. so that they have all the worry of the business, and I can just get paid for what I love doing – I'm no entrepreneur and don't want to be.

6   I want to enjoy it as a hobby and turn to something completely different.

If you choose the last option, you will have lots of different career choices ahead of you but you will need to convince potential employers that you have chosen to follow a different path and that you've researched it properly.

You can enforce your answer to the question above by considering this next question.

What role do you want to play?

The role you aspire to can make a difference to where you position your career and it will be affected by your values. If achievement is important to you, then being a leader, manager or entrepreneur may appeal. If you're a risk taker, then the freelance life may suit you more than if you prefer the security of being an employee. Think about the roles you've played in your life in all the teams you've participated in. Are you a natural leader or do you prefer to be a supportive player? If, within a team, you prefer to support a leader, then running your own business may not be for you. Do you want to be, for example:

* A company owner
  Small business owner
* A leader
  The boss, team leader, self-employed
* Manager
  Project manager, implementing someone's vision, in charge of the budget
* Technician
  Doing the technical aspects as opposed to strategic and business planning
* Support, ensuring everything runs smoothly behind the scenes
  Arts administration, PA in design company
* Entrepreneur
  Creating a business out of a vision
* Freelance support
  Providing a service or product to businesses as and when required

You'll get many people who turn to doing something else and then keep their art and design interests as a hobby. In some cases, this hobby may turn into a full-time occupation, such as designing and crafting greeting cards and calendars. Check out www.docrafts.co.uk for inspiration and networking.

If you're heading down the self-employment and freelance route, how will you handle essential tasks such as agreeing and signing contracts, dealing with health and safety, balancing the books, product and business development, planning your vision and goals for the business, tax, insurance and handling staff?

Do you want to take your creativity and innovative skills into non-related sectors?

Graduates have a wider choice of careers than ever before. This choice has been increasing in length and breadth over the decades, moving from a range of careers for which a degree was essential, such as teachers, medical sciences and veterinary science, to those areas where, increasingly, employers sought graduates as their first choice. Initially, this hit areas such as management, administrative posts in the public and private sector and IT, but recently degrees have been sought by new sectors. Examples include management accountancy, sales and marketing, and buying and purchasing. Many of these have graduate trainee schemes. There are also increasingly the back office support roles in operations and compliance, administration and office management. This is especially as executive assistants and personal assistants increasingly take on the work of junior and middle management.

Many graduates moving into work for which a degree is not required, such as retail, bar and restaurant work and lower-level administrative roles, often do so simply to get started in work, or perhaps in order to save money to go travelling. If you choose to take such a role and you will need to try that much harder to pull yourself out of it if you want to change career or progress. Strategic planning can help you work your way out of it, together with regular self-assessment, plotting, planning, monitoring and reviewing while everyone else parties and sleeps.

Over two-thirds of the vacancies advertised in the year up to the end of July 2004 in *Prospects Today* were for graduates of any degree discipline. This means that you have a wide choice of potential careers, such as marketing, finance, human resources, where your ability to come up with ideas and make things look good will be most welcome or working in general management in commerce or industry. This could open up opportunities for you with large corporates of 5,000+ staff. (Here the application process could move to assessment centres, online applications, psychometric testing and more but the thought of that shouldn't put you off; it should present a challenge.)

Why not bottle, package and sell your creativity as one of your strengths?

Can you come up with ideas, products, services, processes and information which can be applied commercially, or work with people to encourage them to look at old problems through new eyes and approaches? How inventive are you in coming up with new ideas to attract new and retain current customers? Can you create such an experience that the customer will want to come back again and again? Visit www.creative4business.co.uk for inspiration, and read 'Building Enterprise Talent through Employment' at www.starttalkingideas.org which forms part of *The Enterprise Report 2005: Making Ideas Happen.*

Arts and Business in the UK (www.aandb.org.uk) are working to encourage those individuals with creative abilities such as artists to work with businesses to unlock their employees' creativity and capabilities, their passions and values, and to apply them to the way in which they work. Increasing numbers of art and design people are selling their creative skills to companies, enabling them to try different approaches to problems. It has links to all the regions in the UK.

What results do you want?

Results can be viewed in terms of what you achieve through your efforts, and your *rewards* for your work. Both affect you motivation to do the job and your happiness in it. Table 2.1 shows the sorts of results people get at work. Do any of them particularly relate to you?

These questions are important because if you decide to go into a design company, you need to think about the sorts of clients you'll be dealing with.

Table 2.1

Clinching the deal	Exceeding targets
Highest takings	Influencing individuals
Greatest number of arrests	New policy/procedure
A profit	Recognition (from whom?)
Influencing groups	Justice
Strong motivated team	Highest number of commissions
Idea going into fruition	A new approach
Influencing the direction of some-	Happy customers
thing	Famous for what I do
A new look	Huge profits
Recommendations put in effect	Group effort
Take-over of a company	Building relationships/businesses
A sale	Making a difference to a country
Regular exhibitions (and sales)	Making a difference to the world
Money	Seeing your ideas in action
Helping an individual	Other
Making an immediate impact	

What skills do you want to use, i.e. what do you want to do all day?

This can be particularly useful if you would like to change career altogether and move away from art and design; but even so, the exercise will help you pinpoint your strengths and skills you particularly want to use at work.

- Look back over your life experience to achievements you particularly enjoyed. What were you doing when you did them? Examples may include counselling a student or a friend, promoting a concert, teaching English, spotting opportunities or closing a deal or sale.
- What skills do you particularly enjoy using now?
- What skills would you like to feature strongly in your career? (You don't have to stick to those you know – you can learn new skills.)
- What sorts of careers involve these skills?
- In what capacity do you wish to use the skills you've acquired through your degree studies? Look back through your course and pinpoint them. How could you link them all together in a career? What would the picture look like if you were doing them on the job?

If you've got drive and creative talents, there are plenty of opportunities within the creative industries. So what do you want to do? Table 2.2 gives plenty of examples of skills.

Do you want a career in research?

Do you want to further your knowledge and research skills? There are currently over 20,000 people engaged in research in the UK alone. Many work on a project full time, or combine research with other responsibilities such as lecturing or clinical practice, often with others in the UK or abroad. Researchers are also often employed by research councils, the government and other relevant organisations to fulfil various responsibilities such as management, policy advice and project planning. As well as considering the usual academic routes, find out what bodies such as Regional Development Agencies (www.englandsrdas.com) are doing in your sector to support the movement of knowledge and ideas out of their scholastic world

Table 2.2

Achieving	Evaluating	Presenting
Acquiring	Finding solutions	Pricing
Administering	Fundraising	Problem solving
Advising	Guiding	Processing
Analysing	Helping	Producing
Answering	Identifying	Programming
Applying	Implementing	Project management
Assembling	Influencing	Promoting
Assessing	Innovating	Qualitative skills
Building	Inspiring	Quantitative skills
Buying	Interviewing	Questioning
Caring	Inventing	Recommending
Challenging	Investigating	Researching
Classifying	Keeping records	Securing
Coaching	Learning	Selecting
Cold calling	Liaising	Selling
Communicating	Listening	Servicing
Conducting	Locating	Setting targets
Conserving	Making	Studying
Consulting	Managing	Summarising
Counselling	Marketing	Supervising
Creating	Mentoring	Supporting
Critical thinking	Monitoring	Taking risks
Dealing	Motivating	Talking
Debating	Negotiating	Teaching
Designing	Networking	Teamworking
Detecting, e.g. false	Numeracy	Training
logic	Operating	Understanding
Developing	Organising	Watching
Diagnosing	Persuading	Winning
Displaying	Planning	Writing
Distributing	Preparing	Other

and into industry and commerce through the commercialisation of research into spin-out companies. (A spin-out company is created by a university when research generates a product which is commercially viable.) These agencies may be targeting specific industries or 'cluster groups' which they see as having particularly strong potential for economic growth in their region.

The Research Assessment exercise means that the higher education funding bodies can distribute funds for research on quality. Find out more by visiting www.rae.ac.uk for information on the Research Assessment Exercise 2008; and www.hero.ac.uk/rae for the 2001 results. Ratings range from 1 to 5* and it gives an idea of the standard of UK research. See Further Reading and Useful Addresses at the end of this book. The normal route into research is to undertake a post-graduate course (see Chapter 3 for more information).

What's of key importance to you in the career you may choose?

Regardless of the careers you have in mind right now, identify the elements of work which are key to you in your future such as shown in Table 2.3.

Some sectors in the workplace carry particularly unsociable working conditions which go with the territory. In the creative industries, pay is a bit below other sectors and many opportunities are on a freelance, part-time or short-term basis, so you need to develop strong self-promotion and networking skills, and ensure that your skills are updated regularly so that you can use the latest technology. Visit sites such as wwwskillset.org for more information.

Moving your self-awareness forward

Once you've started to identify what's important to you, you can start really focusing on how that relates to the different sectors and opportunities in the workplace.

You can find more careers information about this sector by visiting sites such as:

* Creative and Cultural Skills at www.ccskills.org.uk, which includes profiles of people who've started up their own business. Read *Skills for Creativity* available from the site.

Table 2.3

Motivation	Results/outcomes
Purpose of work	Independence
Location	Entrepreneurship
Contribution to organisation/world/ sector/individuals	Personal fit – feeling that you belong? Skills you use
Sector – matching interests and knowledge	Values, as you identified in Chapter 1 Fit with lifestyle
Rules, ethics and behaviour	Knowledge you use
Role	Creativity
Rewards	Fun
Work for me rather than anyone else	

- www.artsadvice.com – lots of careers information on different opportunities in art and design, with links to more information, plus a helpline you can call for advice.
- www.ideasfactory.com – helping you get to where you want to be in the creative industries, including art and design.
- University of the Arts Careers Service at www.arts.ac.uk/student/careers/1740.htm – a terrific careers library.
- Your Creative Future at www.yourcreativefuture.org.uk for careers information on a range of creative careers.
- www.theessentialguide.co.uk – for anyone wanting to get into the music and entertainment industry.
- ADAM – at www.adam.ac.uk – Arts, Design, Architecture and Media Gateway – a portal of resources.
- Visit too www.careersfair.com/ – an excellent international resource on careers, events and shows, qualifications, careers and training.

Read too, the *Cox Review of Creativity in Business* at www.hmtreasury.gov.uk/independent_reviews and Charles Leadbetter's *Britain's Creativity Challenge* at www.ccskills.org.uk. Both will help you deepen your insight into how your talents and skills are important to employers and they will open up your mind to new opportunities.

Once you have started to work out where you want to be and what you want to be doing, create your own goal, desired result – whatever you choose to call it. You're far more likely to achieve what you want if it is personal to you, reflects your values and it excites you. Create a clear picture of what life will be like when you achieve it. Write your goal down as specifically as you can, to help you focus, and put it somewhere you can see it every day. Talk about what you do want to do – as opposed to what you don't – as if it were already happening. Bring your vision alive and infuse it with energy and drive. Give it a time limit, so that you have something to work for. Finally, make it sufficiently challenging to stretch you, but realistic. It will be more manageable if you break it down into bits, and work through it step by step.

An example of a long term career goal is:

In 3 years' time, I'll have:
> - got a role in a design company;
> - paid off 40 per cent of my student debt;
> - got a network of friends in London I feel I know really well

In six months' time, I'll have:
> ➤ researched all the firms I want to apply to;
> ➤ signed up with a recruitment company which specialises in design;
> ➤ made the necessary networking contacts;
> ➤ attended my first job interview.

A word on family expectations

Families can play a key role in our future career planning, unfortunately sometimes to the detriment of our own judgement of what is right for us. *'I went into it to please my parents'*, often means that graduates went into safe, respectable careers which met with nods of approval and sighs of relief from their family, but made them, the graduate, feel they were en route to jail for a working lifetime. Today, most families are more relaxed about career choice – 'You can't tell them – they make their own minds up!' frequently with all the inference that they still know better. They want us to be safe, protected, happy and successful and a misunderstanding of the job market and a tendency to take on board negative messages from the media makes things worse. There's nothing like the unknown and misunderstood to make people select the safe and known. While our friends and family have our interests very much at heart, their own agendas and self-interest may colour their well-meaning advice to us. They know our qualities well, but may have a limited experience and knowledge of the job market. Pinpoint ways to ask for their help. 'It would really help me if you could ...' and suggest a couple of practical ways they could help. And keep your sights high.

Summary action points

Bringing all the answers to the exercises in this chapter together.

1   What sort of a picture of your future career is emerging? What am I doing in it?
2   What information do I need to firm this picture up?
3   What do I need to happen next to help me further my career plans?
4   What do I need to know to start making decisions?

Chapter 3

Working out the 'how to'

This chapter is all about the 'how'.

How will you get to where you want to be? What could you do to reach the outcome you want? What will you do to position yourself to be in a strong position to make the life you want happen? Figure 3.1 looks at these questions.

Focusing your energies in the right direction with a plan will be a good start, because it will fill your life with vision, purpose and energy, and you'll waste less time on things which aren't important. You can consider all the different ways to get to where you want to be, and to position yourself to follow the best route to make it happen.

As you're deciding on your career, you need to take into account the financial aspects of it all as well and how you're going to start and make it happen. Given that employers are taking people and offering increasingly flexible working patterns (particularly the larger ones), this can work to your advantage. You may need to take a long-term five-year view to give yourself time to create a portfolio or build up an exhibition. But you may get a break far faster than that simply through networking in the right places, winning a competition which brings your name to the forefront of the industry, or bringing a product to events such as the New Designers' Show which hits the mark and wins you interest and contracts. Plot a strategy, and then position yourself to make sure it happens for you and that you tap the right sources of help along the way.

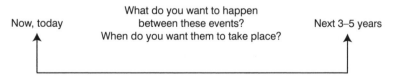

Figure 3.1

What could your next steps be?

Your next steps could involve all or any of those shown in Figure 3.2. The steps shown in Figure 3.2 may *all* feature at some time in your working life, alone or in combination. They may just appear as an opportunity too good to miss. Right now, you may feel like a complete break from academia and work, and head off for six months' break. But if you're truly passionate about what you do at work, it could be hard to cut yourself off from the sector while you're away, and you may find yourself tapping into new networks and being drawn like a magnet to social situations where some instinct tells you that you'll discover like-minded people.

Art and design students who follow a career in their subject in particular, have a fairly fragmented working life, involving stints of permanent employment, time spent developing their own portfolio or studio work, freelancing, temping to get some money, undertaking commissions, further study and unemployment. Many of these feature in the lives of all of us, regardless of degree subject, educational status or career. Although many graduates start out with very definite career aims in mind, they often find they need to become more flexible and move into industries allied to those they originally sought to work in.

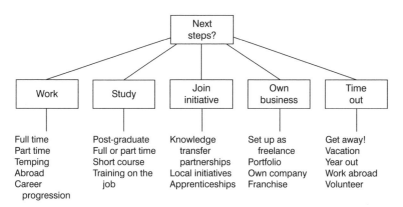

Figure 3.2

What steps do you need to take to fulfil your long-term career and life goals?

One of the first things you need is a vision, especially if you're setting up your own business. Imagine filming yourself on video at work immediately after university, then wind the film forward to three to five years' time. Where are you and what are you doing? Your answers will help you plot your path to success by breaking the longer period down into manageable chunks and tackle them one by one. It's easier to then focus on where you're headed.

Develop an idea, create a vision, do your homework and research the market thoroughly, and make your decision.

Going it alone

Running your own business is about fulfilling your own dreams and not those of someone else. For many, working for someone else deadens their creativity, freedom, independence, fun and being able to work when you want at what you want. There is considerable help for start-ups, from innovative centres where you can hire an office and share facilities at inexpensive rates, to advice from business advisers, events and online sites designed to help you make all the right decisions. Of all graduates, those from creative arts courses are most likely to set up their own business, with craft, music and fine art topping the self-employment table. Take advice: networking clubs can help you talk to fellow entrepreneurs and help each other. In September 2004, Chancellor Gordon Brown launched the National Council for Graduate Enterpreneurship (www.ncge.org.uk). It in turn has set up Flying Start (www.flyingstart-ncge.com) and backed by One NorthEast, the area's regional development agency. It has one-day events, an online community and short residential programmes. You could come up with an idea for a product to sell (such as glassware) or become a freelance, taking on contract work and charging your services out at an hourly or daily rate to companies.

You could buy a franchise, which is a tried and tested product or set up a business selling products. The British Franchise Association (see Useful Addresses at the end of this book) is the only independent accreditation body for franchising in the UK. Franchises cover a wide range of areas from pet care to refill printer cartridges, art suppliers to training centres. There are also workshops and seminars to give you lots of advice and tips on choosing a franchise and running a successful business. Before you buy any franchise, check its financial status and insist on seeing the accounts from its head office. The website www.careersfair.com has details of links to franchises in Italy, France, the USA, Canada, Australia and New Zealand, to name a few.

Self-employment is not the rosy picture it often appears to be. Many small companies are being increasingly strangled by red tape and the compensation culture, and it can be a very lonely affair. You need to put the art, craft or design element aside and consider how you'll handle tasks such as planning the vision for your business, writing a business plan, setting yourself financial targets, dealing with health and safety issues, accounting and financial responsibilities, taking on staff and keeping to the right side of the law, keeping the books and records, on-going business development, product and service development, dealing with the taxman, accountant and suppliers. There are lots of short courses designed to help you handle this, and many art, craft and design websites have further resources as well as business advice or helplines.

Consider the following questions:

- What do you want your business to achieve? What do you want it to do?
- What will it look like in five years' time?
- What financial targets will it meet in six months', one year, three years and five years?
- Who will your customers/clients be? Where will they come from?
- What will your unique selling points be?
- What position will you take in the market?
- What brand do you want? What values will your business portray?
- What will your reputation be based on?
- What message and language can you use to grab potential customers' attention?
- What story would a SWOT analysis give you? (A SWOT analysis looks at Strengths, Weaknesses, Opportunities and Threats facing a business.)
- How does that analysis compare with your competitors in the market?

- What can you do to give your product or service that extra special added value, or to please and surprise your customer or client?
- Where will you run the business from?
- How will running a business impact on your lifestyle?

There will also be key operational questions to ask such as:

- What funding do you need right now to set up and give yourself an income?
- How will you structure the business (e.g. limited company, sole trader, partnership)?
- How will you market your products and services?
- How will you price your products and services?
- What equipment will you need to get started?
- How soon can you get yourself up and running?

If you don't know how to go about any of these things, remember that university has given you the ability *to find them out*. When you started university, you asked where things were, who you needed to talk to in order to get a, b and c done. You knew nothing about the place when you started but you quickly learnt the ropes and found out what you needed to know to make the most of your university days. You can do this again. The website www.artquest.org.uk has an excellent seven-step guide to becoming self-employed, together with a recommended reading list.

Time management and the ability to change focus will be essential if you want to work on a full or part-time basis while building your portfolio and establishing yourself

---

You need to discipline yourself and be swift to adapt from the day job to your real passion, and not waste any time slumping in front of the television for a 30 minute break which can then last the entire evening. A sharp 30–40 minutes' exercise, meditation or yoga can do wonders for clearing your mind and re-energising your mind, soul and body before you switch from one job to to the other. Find a pattern which works for you. If you work well in the morning, do a couple of hours while the rest of the country sleeps and then go out to the day job knowing you've already made headway in your real job. It makes you feel positive. Do some work every single day

– never leave it, because once you do so once, you're more likely to do it for two or three days on the trot, and then you lose the momentum.

Working while developing your own business

Many artists and designers take any job going to bring in some money while they are working to build up their portfolio and prepare for exhibitions. Herein lies a dilemma. It is not uncommon for people to have two or even three jobs at the same time. Many workers in the UK moonlight, doing their bread-and-butter job in the day, and selling merchandise or key skills over the Internet or phone at night. In many cases, these efforts will become full-time businesses. There is the opportunity to work at one thing while looking to achieve a long-term goal doing something totally different. This means that an individual has a divided loyalty which can create stresses and strains, as you change from one culture and role in your paid employment and then come through your front door and switch over to your own special aspirations, goals and the reality of making them work for you.

Can you combine setting up a business with temping?

People temp for many reasons. You could do it to give yourself time to decide what to do, using its flexibility to build your portfolio, making contacts, getting a foot in the door of the industry you want to work in. You can also use it to pick up lots of ideas for your own business, watching how businesses do things, considering how design can help companies grow or not and help people work more effectively together. It can be helpful to sharpen up your business skills and approach and give the way you handle your own affairs a more professional and crisper image.

Temporary work may offer flexibility but it does not guarantee you a regular income. The time you spend worrying about whether you'll have work next week may well be better devoted to your craft. It will, however, put you right into the heart of the workplace, enabling you to build up a web of contacts around a number of companies. You'll quickly find that you're not the only one doing a day job and then getting home to focus on their 'main' job. On the other hand, temping may enable you to take a week off (unpaid) to prepare for that exhibition. You'll need to be able to cope well with uncertainty and swift changes to your day, if this is the route you take.

If you choose to temp through an agency, remember that first and foremost they are businesses seeking to make a profit, so take responsibility for plotting and planning your own career. Whatever reason you temp for, keep your eye on the goal you're aiming for. The *danger* of temping is that you could still find yourself temping after a year, with no further progress in your decision making. Don't allow your own ambitions and aspirations to get lost in the process.

What about getting permanent work?

The good news is that more employers are offering increasingly flexible opportunities and ways to work, such as the three-day week, or a four-day week (ten hours over four days), or night working at an enhanced rate; leaving your days free (don't forget you need to catch up on your sleep). These may give you the assurance you need that the money is coming in, leaving you free to focus on your goal in the holidays, weekends and any spare time you have. But to sell yourself effectively, you need a vision, a mission, a goal, perhaps a niche – call it what you will, which you can break down into manageable chunks, so that every time you achieve a chunk, you feel that you're really making progress to your overall goal. People will want to know all about you and what you're trying to achieve, and your passion and excitement will rub off on them. Build up a database of contacts and you can email them information about your exhibition in a newsletter a couple of weeks prior to it.

Whatever you do to earn money while you're starting out, a strong focus on your most important goals will be the key to success, with lots of energy and a strong vision of where you're headed in the future.

What further learning do you need to undertake to get to where you want to be?

There are various forms of learning: informal, where you find the information you need to mug up on and learn about it yourself; and the more formal, set in short or longer courses. Identify what you need to know or have expertise in to be successful in the work you want to do, find out where you can get this learning and what you need to apply for it (resources, financial, knowledge, talent etc.) and then do it. One of the first ideas which may occur to you is doing a post-graduate degree.

To be ... a post-graduate or not?

Post-graduate courses come in different guises. There's a course designed to enhance and deepen your knowledge in a particular area, such as an MA in Ceramics or Children's Book Illustration. You could take a course which will help springboard you into a career area, such as Museum Management. Alternatively, you could enrol for research-based studies, such as a PhD (Doctor of Philosophy), in subjects such as Twentieth-Century French Art History which take about three or four years full time to complete and which can take you into the field of research, perhaps for a university, private organisation, institute or research project. Some post-graduate degrees involve an element of teaching and research.

Some employers sponsor employees through degree and post-graduate courses and may even approach a university to create a bespoke course and qualification for their employees. Equally, some people study a post-graduate degree for their own (career) development, perhaps part time or online. People study post-graduate degrees for various reasons, to boost their career prospects or to simply increase their specialist knowledge and expertise in a particular area. Many students work for several years before taking a full-time post-graduate degree. By this time, they can envisage exactly how that study will fit into longer-term career plans, plus they've got experience to talk about when they finally come to getting that post-graduate job. Timing is tricky: leave it too long and it may be too late to put impetus and fresh energy into your career.

Questions to consider before you sign up for a post-graduate degree

1   How does this course take you closer to achieving your long-term career plans? Where does it fit in with them?

2   Will a post-graduate degree substantially boost your chances of success? Will it really give you that edge over your competitors? What do employers think?

3   Are you contemplating post-graduate study simply to put off joining the working world for another year? (The longer you leave it, the harder it may be.)
4   What are the costs and what funding is available?
5   What have post-graduate students gone on to do after their studies? How do these paths relate to your aspirations?
6   What will it take to be a successful applicant and student?
7   What are your motivations for taking such a course (entry into a new career, career progression)?

Is it really a post-graduate course you need, or would another form of study and learning be more appropriate for the skills and knowledge you seek? Be specific about your learning needs.

What evidence do you have that post-graduate study will enhance your employment prospects? Could networking and getting the right experience under your belt, perhaps by doing an internship, be as effective? Weigh up your options and talk to professionals in the field before you decide what to do.

Further information on post-graduate studies

You'll find the official UK post-graduate database at www.prospects.ac.uk which lists the different courses available by subject, region and institution in the UK. It gives research specialisms, RAE ratings, number of students, duration of course, contact details and, importantly, the programme aims, including how the level of importance areas such as vocational/occupational training, professional development, research and scholarship, and preparation for research. It is worth noting that an increasing number of post-graduate courses can be studied online or part time. You can apply online through Prospects, and even use some sections of the application for different courses which will save you time. In the UK, apply as soon as you can because the more popular courses fill up quickly – this means often October or November in the year before the course is due to start. The National Postgraduate Committee (www.npc.org.uk) represents the interests of post-graduate students in the UK.

If you live outside the UK, the British Council (www.britcoun.org) has offices throughout the world and can give you lots of information about studying and living in Britain. The National Academic Recognition Information Centre (NARIC, www.naric.org.uk) provides a service for international students who want information on the comparability between international and UK qualifications.

Short courses may be just the ticket

A short course may boost your employability and give you the skills you need to get the post you want. In the UK, you can find courses at www.hotcourses.com; you could also visit your local college and private training companies to find out what they have to offer. Courses relating to the workplace should include a stint of work experience to give you confidence and practice, and the course tutors should also have strong contacts with employers in the sector. When you have pinpointed what you want to do then, if you are lacking any particular skills, a short course could be just the ticket to close the gap between what you've got and what employers want. A career development loan (www.direct.gov.uk/cdl) may be the last thing you feel like acquiring but, if you live in the EU, it could provide you with the finance you need to fill that vocational skill gap and boost your employability.

Short on skills and business knowledge?

A combination of subjects taken at university may have given you skills and knowledge in areas such as business studies, administration, marketing and public relations. You may be able to pick these up through short courses on offer locally. LearnDirect (www.learndirect.co.uk) offers such courses to small companies. ACAS (www.acas.org.uk) offers a small number of courses on employment law at a very cost-effective rate.

Enrolling for professional qualifications

You may plan to study for professional qualifications once you have decided on the business function you wish to work with. These qualifications give you the core knowledge and competences which you need to perform effectively at work; they give you the theory and practice which gives you a competitive edge. In some industries, you cannot advise clients or practice without them. Working towards them normally involves taking a number of examinations and practical experience. Consider which is best for you (talk about this with your employer, but do some fact finding about professional qualifications as you move through your career decision-making process). Think about how you want to study, be it online, by evening class, through block learning or distance learning. Professional bodies will have a list of accredited training providers and most have a very considerable range of support mechanisms to help you through.

Undertake a skills audit

What further skills do you need to make the leap from where you are now to where you want to be? This could be in areas such as interview technique, practising for assessment centres or CV writing. Alternatively, if you want to run your own business, it could be in subjects such as business functions, customer care, employing staff, health and safety issues, branding and motivating people. What steps can you take to ensure your skills are top notch? What training do you need? This may or may not be sector specific.

Working already?

If you studied part time while working, look back at the reasons why you enrolled for an under-graduate or post-graduate degree. Perhaps you did so with your employer's knowledge, blessing and support. If this is the case, discuss your future with your employer, your direct boss or HR or both. Questions to ask include:

- What do I want to happen next?
- Where do I see my career going in the next five years?
- How do I see myself doing this: with my current employer, with another employer or starting my own business?
- What do I need to do now to make this happen?
- How has my new degree status changed my CV and what I have to offer?

Re-write your CV for your next perfect role, or write a job description for the role you really crave. What is missing from where you are now and where you want to be? Perhaps it's taking on a new project which will give you exposure to a particular experience or new skillset. Ensure there are no other options open to you with your current company. Talk to your line-manager and HR department about the studies you've been doing and find out how the company can best use them. If you don't use them, you'll waste them. Outside of the office, ask yourself if your current employer can help you meet your career aspirations. Your goals may have changed since you started the course; you may want to change career or go it alone, or start afresh with another company. If your employer sponsored you through your degree, did you commit to staying with the company for a given length of time after graduating? If you did, you may need to negotiate an exit.

Whatever you choose to do, stretch your new confidence and intellectual prowess. Work to achieve your potential, not to reduce it because your current role isn't right for you. That may mean cutting the strings with your current employer.

Heading out to job hunt

If you have decided that you want to work for someone else, it's time to start job hunting and networking to boost your chances of success. There are a number of things you can do, such as:

1 Make use of the careers support in your area.
2 Search out professional organisations which can help you build networks leading to introductions in the sectors you need; find out exactly what you will need to do to achieve that cherished professional status you want.
3 Build up a clear picture of the sector you wish to go into and be clear about how your skills, strengths and interests will contribute to it.
4 Find out what is going on to encourage graduates and small companies to get working together.
5 Read the rest of this book which has lots of ideas for networking, hunting out opportunities, making the switch from being a scholar to student and promoting yourself.

'I want to work abroad!'

Working abroad requires considerable research and preparation if you're to have the experience you want. Recruitment companies who have an international reach often have advice on their sites about moving abroad. The website www.asia.hobsons.com has information on working in China, Taiwan, Thailand, Hong Kong,

Singapore, Malaysia, Indonesia and Japan with market trends and industry summaries, and overall regional outlooks plus details of events in the area. Prospects (www.prospects.ac.uk) has numerous country profiles, incorporating details on the job market, international companies in the region you're reading about, language requirements, work experience, vacancy sources and visa and immigration information. See Further Reading at the end of this book for some useful suggestions.

Questions to consider

1   What do you want to get out of the experience? What is your reason for going?
2   Where do you want to work? Do you want to take the opportunity to learn a new language or improve existing language skills?
3   What do you want to do? Do you want to work for an employer in a job which will contribute to your career progression or simply go apple picking for six months?
4   How different do you want the culture of the country you're going to work in to be from your own?
5   How will your current qualifications be regarded in the country you plan to work in – will you need to get any additional 'top up' qualifications to meet their own regulations and criteria to work as a practising professional?
6   What visa requirements will there be? What happens about health insurance? What are the tax implications for you while working abroad and when you return home?
7   Can you do it under the auspices of your current or a future employer?
8   How long do you want to do it for?

Time out for golden sands, sea, sun ...

If you've been on the academic treadmill all your life without a break, you may feel that it's time for some time out, fun and rest. Increasing numbers of people of all ages are taking time out and more (larger) employers are offering employees sabbaticals. They like seeing them return to the workplace refreshed, with a new confidence, fresh ideas, great soft skills and creativity. Gap programmes too are waking up to the fact that more of us want time out, and providing excellent opportunities for voluntary work and travel.

That said, you live your life once. The moment you stop experiencing such adventures as travel and facing challenges in life, you stop living and start existing. Travelling will give you lots of opportunities to collect new ideas and influences, which you can incorporate into your work when you return home. If you plan to take some time out, you could look for a job before you go and try to negotiate a start date for when you return (assuming you will return); or you could travel and look for a job when you get back. This gives you more flexibility and possibly more stress as you wonder how on earth you're going to find a job and pay off your debts when you get home. One possibility is to consider overseas internships and training schemes. See Further Reading at the end of this book.

Unemployment ...

Not a very inspiring option, is it? So get busy.

Seven ways to pass the time while you're unemployed

1   Get relevant work experience, even if it's just for a week or a couple of days a week over a month or so.
2   Do voluntary work.
3   Learn new skills.
4   Travel.
5   Job hunt persistently and seriously.
6   Do something quite mad and quirky to make your CV stand out.
7   Study for a qualification which will give you on-the-job skills.

Acknowledge that this is a difficult time, because you've been through all the hard work towards your graduation, celebrated in style, promised complete strangers you met in the Union Bar in the last 24 hours at university that you'll keep in touch ... and suddenly, it's all over. And it's a strange feeling, so be aware of it and then turn your attention to the future.

If your family are trying to help you but in the wrong way, be patient. They simply want to help you and their intentions are good. Show them how they can help you by saying 'What would really help me is if you could...' It could be they could introduce you to someone whom you need to talk to about a career move into a specific industry.

Give your life a turbo-boost!

If you're currently sitting at home aimlessly with no defined plans or goals and no meaningful way to fill your day, it's time to change that. We all need to feel appreciated – it's a basic human need. Change the way you're spending your time and energy. If you're joining an industry in which contract and freelance work features heavily, you will need to become accustomed to periods of employment between commissions and contracts and develop strong skills in networking and promoting yourself and your talents.

Start climbing out of where you are now and start walking purposefully to where you want to be.

1   Brainstorm strategies you can use which will boost your chances of success, such as a willingness to move and live where the sector is strongest geographically. If you want to stay where you are, where the sector may be weak or even non-existent, be more flexible in terms of the sort of work you go for.
2   Talk to fellow graduates. What sort of business could you start up together based on your mutual interests and passions?
3   Talk to as many people as you can by going to where you know you'll find them, outside the usual graduate arena, such as trade exhibitions and local networking events.
4   Set yourself daily targets and goals in every area of your life, not just your career. Life isn't just about work.

Summary action points

Move your thinking forward:

1   Which university or college runs the course in the subject I'm looking for?
2   What funding is available for me to set up my own business?
3   What initiatives are available that might be relevant to me and my career goals?
4   What do I need more of in my life? How can I get it?
5   What steps will I take next and how will they move me closer to my goals? What do I need to do to make them happen?

Chapter 4

Connecting with your network

The world's a network

Connecting to those in the know who can help you move closer to the things you want in life will enable you to enjoy a far richer life and career. Chapters 4 and 5 will help you pinpoint people who can help you create or open doors to new opportunities.

A strong, active network can open doors to decision makers and in turn enable you to reach out, help others and live a highly successful and fulfilling life. Whatever stage of life and career you are at, it will enhance your prospects of obtaining the introductions you need. Highly successful people have a network of business associates, acquaintances, colleagues and friends they can turn to for information, advice, introductions and help. You create your own luck and networks in life, however, and they are as active and useful and productive as you make them. Remember that networking is also about helping those who *have* helped you, and those who *haven't*.

This chapter considers the *Who* question in a networking capacity.

1 *Who* can help me?
2 *Who* can give me the support I need now?
3 *Which* websites will be most useful?

Eight steps to successful networking

1 An ability to chat and be really interested in the other person; you need to be able to establish a rapport with strangers quickly.
2 Listening and questioning skills.
3 A get-up-and-go attitude – go out there and fight for your place in the world.

4   Follow through. Use the information you acquire, file it for future thought, action it or dump it, but *do* something with it.
5   Lateral thinking – does your contact know of anyone else you
should talk to?
6   Respect! The person you're talking to has got to where they
are by hard work. They believe in what they are doing and in
what the job stands for. It may not turn out to be your niche or
world, but respect them for what they love about theirs.
7   Being inquisitive and curious.
8   Accept feedback calmly.

You may not always like what you hear. Challenge the person
giving feedback politely. *'This is a very tough industry and not many
people make it to the starting blocks.'* Okay, so that may be the case,
but clearly people *do* need to make it so you need to focus on that
percentage – whatever it is – the 5, 10, 20 per cent of applicants
– and find out just what it is that brings them success. Focus on
the people who've succeeded, not on generalisations that *'It's difficult, it's tough'*. It may well be, but it's not impossible. Turn the
negatives around to: *'It's difficult, but it's possible. It's tough but
it's rewarding.'* Talk about the *'I can'* and *'I will'* rather than the *'I'll
try'* or *'Maybe…'*. Ask people *'What is your perception of me?'* to
get feedback on how you present yourself and how you come over.
This will help give them something to remember you by. *'I met with
a designer who was absolutely passionate about … really great ideas
and done some terrific projects. You should give them a call – might
be able to help you …'*.
    What would be the cost to you if didn't achieve your career
goals? Envisaging such an outcome can provide a terrific leverage to
get you out of your comfort zone and make those phone calls and
send the emails to make contacts. It can propel you into making that
extra effort, going the extra mile and turning the last corner to find
the right opening. What are you prepared to do in order to make
sure it happens? How outlandish are you prepared to be in the way
you tackle a situation, and how far out of your comfort zone are you
prepared to go to make it happen? Your passion for your career and
what you want to achieve should inspire and excite you so much
that you're prepared to do what it takes to sell yourself. True networking is only really effective when you push yourself out of your
comfort zone and think out of the box.

A key benefit to your networking activities will be to create and build a strong support team around you. Each person on your team should bring you something different. There will be members of your support team you've known all your life, such as your family, family friends and your friends. Within that group, there will be one or two people whom you trust perhaps just that little bit more than the rest. You know they will be open and honest with you and you also know you handle any constructive criticism from them because it's fair and just. Then there are people who fill you with energy, a 'can do' approach, who could inspire you to great things. Perhaps these may include your peers at university; how often have you sat about and brainstormed an idea late into the night which is going to make you all lots of money and bring you fame? Keep in regular contact with those friends who enable you to unlock your potential and your creativity. There will also be the people you (secretly) admire and consider your success and role models. They may be a member of your family, perhaps your mother or father; or they could be a high profile leader in business, politics, the community or someone with a 'go ahead' approach which fills you with energy and passion for your own beliefs and causes. Bring these people on board by studying their methods to achieve success. What did they sacrifice along the way to get to where they wanted to be? How did they focus? Why not contact them to ask them how they did it and what advice they have for you? Would they even act as a mentor to you? Finally, there are those who are not yet known to you – those people working in the sort of profession you want to be in, those who can advise you and help you along the way. It is here that the skill of networking truly comes into its own.

The benefits of networking

Networking is all about asking others to help you access information which will help you – or others – get to where you need to be. You can access information and decision makers. You can tap into those in the know who are most likely to know the answer you need – it's a bit like the 'phone a friend' lifeline on the UK television programme *Who Wants to be a Millionaire?* The contestants choose the friend who is mostly likely to know the answer to the question they are faced with, and it's the same here. You need to reach those beyond those you know and extend a line and call for information and help to those you *don't*.

This is the same in life. We all need the right people to call on in moments of crisis because we know they will give us the right support at that moment. We choose our friends because they have qualities we admire and enjoy. We elect to take some family members into our confidence as opposed to others because we know they have something slightly different to offer us, perhaps due to their life experience or their approach or attitude. As we go through life, we'll call on people at different times and there will be periods when we aren't in touch at all. Nonetheless, keep those fires of warmth and support burning because we know that when the time comes, we'll need to know we can pick up the telephone and call them or drop them an email to ask for help, even if it's just a friendly ear. Just the same way, there are people who know they can call on us.

Let's consider how networking can help you in your career. If you brainstorm all the people you know, who you've met or watched at presentations as they came into your university, you can probably draw up a long list, as shown in Figure 4.1.

Fifteen ways networking can help you in your career

1   Acquiring relevant work experience, especially in highly competitive sectors where contacts are everything.
2   Help with your CV, application or portfolio.
3   Information about a career or organisation, or better still, an introduction to someone working in it.
4   An idea of the skills, qualities and experience an employer wants and the personalities they recruit; would you be a good 'fit'?
5   How a sector works, e.g. the culture, behaviour, dress, language, values.
6   The name of the best recruitment agency for you to talk to.
7   Advice on the best way 'in' to a sector or company.
8   Projects an employer needs doing but does not have the resource internally to undertake which you could then volunteer for.
9   Tip-offs when a job comes up – many companies advertise their vacancies to staff first on their notice boards or company intranet.
10   What roles are available for new graduates?
11   Where is the best place to look for vacancies?

In the sector you want to work in:

- within a company
- across different companies in the sector
- universities to find out what's new and hot on the knowledge front
- university to university, if you're an academic
- professional bodies
- organisations devoted to the sector e.g. Arts Council
- cluster groups, on a national, regional and local basis
- graduate initiatives, e.g. Knowledge Transfer Partnership
- links between universities and employers

Networks dedicated to start-up businesses or helping graduates:

- the self-employed and small business networks such as the Federation of Small Businesses
- government bodies, e.g. BusinessLink
- cross-cultural networks and organisations
- organisations targeted at particular groups, e.g. Women In Rural Enterprises
- sector specific networks
- government agencies

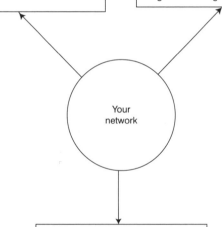

Your network

Personal networks:

- leisure and hobby interests
- voluntary and public sectors
- community service organisations, e.g. Soroptimists (women) and Rotary International
- friends and family
- professionals, e.g. doctors, dentists
- product and service providers you use, e.g. banks, builders, garages, etc.
- school, college, university
- religious organisations
- fellow students – could you do something together?

Figure 4.1

12   Discussing the industry overall, its strengths, weaknesses, opportunities and threats; the pros and cons of working in it and how it is structured.

13   Advice from small business owners as they reflect back on their own experiences of setting up. Did they make any mistakes they would warn others about?

14   Names of bodies and groups who are really helpful when setting up a business.

15   Names of grants or funding you can tap into.

Many people don't push their network into unknown areas so never really truly reap the benefits networking can bring.

The danger of networking with fellow graduates is that if you're both in the same boat, you may simply spend time and energy bemoaning the current state you're in, which won't change anything. So if you're talking to a fellow graduate, have a good moan for five minutes and then spend 15 minutes brainstorming in which you can both change the situation you're in for the better and bounce ideas and contacts off each other. One of those ideas could be the breakthrough you've been looking for.

Get pushy and ask for help – most people will be delighted to help you

Six steps to pro-active networking

1   Identify what you need to know or what sort of people you want to meet and why they are important to you.

2   Identify the people you *do know* and imagine on paper what their network would be like.

3   Make contact and ask for advice and help. If someone has referred you to a contact, mention their name.

4   Approach people you don't know but can find more easily through relevant professional organisations and trade associations.

5   Think big and laterally and you could connect to thousands of people worldwide at a stroke. The key is to secure introductions to the people in the right place.

6   Be open to asking for advice and help.

Professional organisations

Professional bodies exist partly to help promote the public's confidence in the professions they represent. As such, membership of a professional body may be essential to practice. They also help members and new entrants into the field to have satisfying and fulfilling careers, access to the right training and networks, and meet the challenges and opportunities that come their way. Many such organisations in the creative industries are listed under Useful Addresses at the back of this book. Their sites may cover such topics as shown in Table 4.1.

Most professional organisations are sympathetic to the job seeker, especially those from college or university, or returning to work. On initial contact, you may talk to a person employed by the professional body to be at the end of the phone, offering information and advice. They will have particular hints and advice for you, the new entrant, the career changer, the mature student and the young professional. They can also help point you in the direction of areas of their website which may be of interest and to local groups in your area.

As an example, in the UK, the Association of Illustrators (AOI) has different categories of membership, catering for working illustrators, those not yet commissioned, students in full-time education and corporate members (agents and clients). Each category has its own fee structure, facilities and services. Examples of these services include a dedicated phone line for legal and pricing advice, a

Table 4.1

• A register of practitioners and their areas of expertise and specialism, often with their contact details	• Career case studies
	• Learning and education
	• Useful links
• Events taking place at which members, associates and affiliates may gather	• Information about the profession as a whole
	• Library services
• Jobs search	• Annual conferences in the UK and abroad
• Online forum groups	• Salary calculator
• Latest industry news	• Services available to the public
• Latest publications relevant to the industry	• Vacancy listings
	• Advice line on pricing issues
• Research	• Setting up on your own
• Information for the public on the body, its standards, ethics and training	

substantial discount on portfolio surgeries with a professional consultant and discounts on art materials. Pricing and legal advice can be particularly invaluable for the illustrator just starting out.

Professional bodies' discussion forums are very useful to see what the hot topics are and to be able to comment on them at interviews or assessment days. It is not uncommon for people to ask for careers advice and point out that they are looking to move into an area, and for other professionals to come forth with advice and information. Many organisations have local networks, with regular meetings (sometimes with a speaker), events, training programmes and newsletters. There may also be visits to businesses for a look around, or a social gathering. Most will enable members to talk to each other and catch up, meet new people or give each other referrals.

Go on – attend a meeting in your area

It is in the organisation's best interests to show you goodwill and interest and yours to represent yourself in a professional manner. Dress in business attire – suit and tie – and practice good social skills – a warm, firm handshake, a smile and lots of eye contact. Ask questions – what people do, who do they work for, what sort of clients do they have? If they give you their business card, follow it up with an email saying something like 'It was nice to meet you – would it possible for us to meet up? – I'd love to talk you further about …' Be ready to talk positively about your course, the projects you did and that you are currently working on, your career plans,and people who inspire you. Mention articles you've seen in the press or online which show you're up-to-date and show enthusiasm and interest. Find out before you go about any initiatives in your area which are running to strengthen the relationship between graduates and small employers – it could just help swing the mind of a small employer to give a graduate like you a chance, if only he or she had some guidance on how to make the most of you.

If the thought of attending such a meeting fills you with horror...

Why not contact the person in charge of your local group to explain that you're coming along for the first time and to ask for someone to look out for when you arrive to introduce yourself to? There should be someone there whose role it is to welcome new members and make them feel at home. Look out for them, and ask them to introduce you to someone who is working in a specific area that you'd like to get involved with. Find out in advance who will be there, and head for those you most want to talk to when you arrive, armed with prepared questions. Be interested and you'll soon forget your own nerves. Remember that you're with a group of like-minded people who may well remember what it's like to start out. They're on your side. Ask to meet them to find out more. Identify specific questions to ask before you go so that it is clear you have given the meeting some thought and prepared well for it.

Join your alumni

Do it now; you'll find details on your university's website. Try tracking down past alumni who are working in sectors you want to join. They can answer many of your questions, give you advice and may be able to point you in the right direction for more help and support. Find out what they like and dislike about what they're doing, and what they see the challenges are from the point of view of their career and life. What appealed to them about the organisation they joined and how has the partnership fared so far? Where do they see it going in the future? Why not set up an e-group (you can do this through *Yahoo*, for example) of your fellow graduates to act as a focal point of ideas, contacts, support, advice and help?

Academic groups

Academics network across the world as much as professionals in the business field. They attend conferences, listen to papers, give presentations, undertake joint research projects, compare notes, research, debate, argue, discuss, discover and invent. They talk on the phone, they email and they have their own networks across their universities, research institutes and other relevant organisations. They live and breathe their subjects, and they're encouraged to work with business, whether they like it or not, and to create a far more entrepreneurial spirit in their departments and students.

You may be thinking that academic life is for you. Visit websites such as www.jobs.ac.uk for information on jobs in the higher education sector and check their institutions' own websites for vacancies. As well as academic posts, universities also need staff in areas such as finance, marketing, public relations, administration, student support, human resources and facilities and building management.

Informal networks

As important as their formal peers, informal networks are the places to go to meet like-minded people who will cheer you up when you feel low, give you good, sound advice over a pint and talk about *the* latest design from the sector which is truly giving everyone the 'Wow!' factor. You may find these networks in coffee houses, bars, restaurants, art galleries, pubs – any place where people in the sector hang out. You can also tap into informal networks through any social situation; remember that talking to an accountant over a drink, he may have clients in the sector who just could provide that right introduction for you. Be chatty and interested, passionate and enthusiastic, keen and self-motivated and you'll attract help and support, but remember that you may need to go out of your way to find it.

What about websites?

You can network and access careers advice and information online and in person through a number of sites and these are listed under Useful Addresses through university careers services and government providers, plus sites such as www.prospects.ac.uk and www. hobsons.ac.uk. Wherever you are, visit or contact your local university's careers service and find out what help is available to you as a new graduate. Be specific about the help you need. Go into careers interviews knowing what you want to cover. Be honest with yourself and others – this is not a test. In addition, there may be sites geared towards graduates in your particular region, such as GradSouthWest (www.gradsouthwest.com) in the southwest of the UK (see Useful Addresses at the back of this book).

Sector specific networks

Websites in themselves can be invaluable, particularly if you use them to signpost you towards other sites. It's worth checking national government websites such as www.culture.gov.uk (the Department for Culture, Media and Sport in the UK). Delve too into local government and initiatives such as www.creativeherefordshire.

co.uk and www.creativeyorkshire.com; these will tend to have details of help on offer in the area, advice for those starting out, details of trade shows, training, events, help-lines, agencies and links. They focus fully on the creative industries so you really are honing in on what matters to you.

There are also international bodies such as the International Federation of Interior Architects/Interior Designers (www.ifiworld.org), and national organisations such as the Arts Council and the Design Council in the UK, and their equivalents elsewhere. Again, many of these are listed under Useful Addresses at the back of this book. Some of these are country *and* sector specific, such as www.fashion-fromspain.com.

Some nations are spearheading groups to promote and develop training and development in different sectors on three levels: first, to help employers ensure that they have the trained and skilled staff they need to fulfil their business goals and vision; secondly, to help those seeking to start up their own businesses; and thirdly, to help individuals maximise their potential. For example, national training organisations and bodies such as Skillset (www.skillset.org) which has seven screen academies. There are also bodies such as www.creativeclusters.com designed to help employers find the business support they need. There are also a number of sites – often put together by governments or bodies – to help businesses understand how designers can work to help them promote their products and services (www.betterbydesign.org.nz in New Zealand is an example). It helps companies there make world-class design a big difference for their products and services in the export market.

There are non-government related organisations such as www.a-n.co.uk, the Artists Professional Information Company, with information for subscribers on awards, competitions, art vacancies, opportunities, the employment market and running your own business. Another example is www.i10.org.uk, the i10 cultural and creative industries network, an online zone which enables you to access news and events, facilities, graduate jobs and technology transfer opportunities. Check out too www.ideasfactory.com – the site provides useful links and opportunities to converse with others in the creative industries.

For regional help, a great source of useful links is http://www.apd-network.info/members_frames.html. This amazing page will take you straight to sources of help throughout the UK, into its very corners. There are details of art and design support organisations in

London, the North West, East London, Cornwall, Wales, Glasgow, Herefordshire, Sheffield, Suffolk, the North East, Yorkshire, Portsmouth and more. These sites can lead you to networks and professional development programmes, including one-to-one seminars, critical conversations, marketing and networking opportunities, the chance to share information and advice, and access to research facilities, funding and business support.

Some websites are very specific. For example, www.advantagecreativefund.co.uk has details of those looking for investment or help in order to grow their creative business in the West Midlands. Use the links and further information sections of websites to delve further. Talk to people who have succeeded – is there a particular body, group or individual they found especially useful when they were setting up? More sites are listed under Useful Addresses at the back of this book.

Start-ups

There are also websites for the small businesses and start-ups, such as the Federation of Small Businesses (www.fsb.org.uk) , the Small Business Service, Start-Ups and BusinessLink. They can all signpost you in the right direction. These will enable you to make friends and potential clients, customers or employers over the Internet. Again, some are very specific, such as Women in Rural Enterprises (WIRE) in the UK (see www.wireuk.org). Think laterally.

Networking outside your sector

This is important if you wish to gain new clients. If you're running a small business or freelance service, you need to decide how to promote your services. In this instance, you could consider attending local events put on to help business people network and exchange business cards so that they can pick up on each other's services and how they may help businesses. Local networking events targeting small businesses may help. Explore the networks in your area and on the Internet, and assess which ones will be most appropriate to you.

Successful networking

Open-mindedness and generosity is crucial, but be discerning too. Listen to what people have to say, and then assess the information and feedback you're getting against what's important to *you* and your criteria.

Ten more steps to successful networking

1 Don't assume the information you're getting is current. Don't assume those you're talking to are up-to-date. Go that extra mile to check with professional bodies and trade associations.
2 Guard your safety. If you're meeting someone, do so in a public place or in their office premises. Visit the company's website to make sure their address is valid. Don't give too many personal details out over the Internet or telephone.
3 Present yourself to the highest standard possible using business behaviour and language. Dress in your interview suit then examine your image from head to toe in front of a long mirror at home. If you're self-employed, think about the image you want to portray about your business.
4 Use networking to digest strategies which will put you ahead of the competition, whether you're looking for a new job or starting and developing your own business.
5 Networking is a two-way process. When people help you, see if there is anything you can do to help them. Build on the relationships you develop. Treat others as you would like to be treated yourself.
6 If you are at a networking event, spend about five minutes talking to the person you're with and then move on. You are *all* there to meet as many people as possible, so close the conversation. *'It's been nice to meet you. Shall we exchange cards and move on?'*
7 What perception do you want the people you meet to have of you? Do you want to come over as someone who takes their career and chosen field seriously and passionately, or as someone who's out to have a good time? Are you portraying yourself to be someone who can be trusted and loyal?
8 Don't give the impression that you hop from one company to another. It costs employers money to recruit staff and they won't be too impressed if you arrive, work for a year or so,

and then move on. Word gets around, especially if you live in a small community or work in a small sector. Be discreet if you're looking elsewhere for opportunities.

9   Set yourself goals for each networking opportunity. What do you want to achieve from it? Divide your networks in groups and give each group a goal for the week or month. Measure your success. What are you doing that is yielding the best results?

10 Keep in touch with people in your network. Email them from time to time to ask how they are and how things are going. A network is only as active and alive as you make it.

Business coaches

Career and business coaches help you identify what is important to you, what you want to achieve and what you need to do to make that happen. Some coaches work in a niche, for example, only with small creative companies and individuals to help them achieve their business and personal goals. Check that your coach is qualified and trained and find out what experience he or she has before parting with any money.

Go out there and immerse yourself in the fabric and make-up of those working in the sector you want to get into

Aim to build up a very strong understanding of the world you want to work in and seek to identify who really knows the local scene and has an influence in it. Informal networks are as important as those which are of a professional foundation, so find out where people meet in your sector if you're in a new town and head on down there. It's a great chance to meet with like-minded people who share the same passions you do and they will pull you up when you're feeling low and point you in the direction of all sorts of useful resources.

Networking is for life!

Networking can be very helpful in all sorts of ways including:

1   finding specialist expert health advice;
2   locating the estate agent who will really get your house sold fast and is always the first to hear of houses coming onto the market;
3   getting your children into the right school;
4   looking after ageing relatives and making the system work to your advantage;
5   volunteering to give something back;
6   meeting people of like mind, such as knowing where the places are to go to meet fellow artists and designers;
7   asking about hotels for that special holiday next year;
8   meeting new people at the pub, in the gym and through your interests;
9   learning something new and keeping your life fresh and active;
10 having fun and giving something back at the same time.

Summary action points

The way you network at every level can affect the flavour and fabric in your life so make it a priority.

1   What network groups are there in your area which you can make contact with and get involved with? List them and make that first contact.
2   Find out if they have mentors to help people like yourself who want to get into the sector. If they do, ask if you can be allocated one.
3   Contact five people in your network. Ask if they know of anyone who could help you. Arrange to meet for a coffee to catch up with them or organise an information meeting.

Chapter 5

Hunting out the right opportunity

So far, you've ascertained what you want to do – now you need to work out how and where you want to do it.

How important is the 'Where?' to you?

What factors are driving your decision in terms of where you live? Many UK graduates move abroad to find the lifestyles and career opportunities they want – and what have they got to lose? The choices shown in Table 5.1 can all impact on your future life and the opportunities within it, so consider which option in each line is most important to you. This is also a good test of how important your career is to you compared with the other elements in life. Would you move tomorrow to where the right career opportunities were for you, regardless of where that was?

Other factors which will impact on your lifestyle are your access to cultural activities, sports and leisure interests, the make up of local people and quality of life in the area. You are unlikely to find somewhere which meets all of these criteria so some degree of compromise will be required. If your career matters to you above all else, you'll move to where the sector is strong and growing fast as opposed to where it is non-existent.

What's the global picture?

Visit the website www.creativeclusters.com which can help you pinpoint international creative clusters from various countries such as the Nordic regions, Australia, New Zealand, the USA, Europe and the UK. Some of the links may be rather more theory based, but others have hot tips and advice, such as www.creativefutures.cadise. ac.uk. Many countries are seeking to export their cultures through

Table 5.1

Near friends	Same town as friends	Ready to make new friends and keep in touch with old ones
Close to family	Living with parents	Irrelevant – we email and text and they can visit
Cost of living low	Cost of living irrelevant – salary will match	Need to keep this in mind – must find out what living costs are
Opportunity to live cheaply to pay back loans	Have bills, but then doesn't everyone?	Not as important as the job itself
Sector I want to go into is strong in the region with lots of employers	I'll take my chances – I want to stay in the city I did my degree in. I'll take what I find	I'm ready to go to the other side of the world to get the job I want
Staying in home country	Want to go abroad	If the job takes me abroad, so be it
City	Town	Countryside/rural
Irrelevant – the job comes first	Have a strong preference for where I live	Am absolutely living in this city regardless of opportunities
Short commute to work	Commute is irrelevant – it's the job and employer which matters	Willing to commute within reason
Want to be right in the heart of where it's all happening	Want access to art and design facilities	Am changing career, so not that important to me

various creative means, to give people an experience of them. They also recognise that creativity has true value, and that the value comes from those who have ideas and can apply them commercially through services and manufacturing.

Consequently, countries are investing resources into the sector. In Hong Kong, the Policy Address (www.policyaddress.gov.hk) in 2005 includes new measures to develop the region's cultural and creative industries. In Taiwan, Premier Frank Hsieh has committed NT\$20 billion to go into the creative and cultural industries over the next five years to give them a boost. Lebanon has a five-year programme for developing and supporting the Creative Industries there. In the USA, a Congressional Report has been issued in 2005 regarding the Creative Industries.

What's the picture in the UK?

An essential read is the DTI's paper 'Creativitiy, Design and Business Performance' which sets out clearly the picture in terms of the role of creativity and design in driving business performance and productivity. The Creative Industries account for 5 per cent of the UK's GDP, although about 17 per cent of the industry's businesses suffer from skills shortages, especially business and management skills. Nonetheless, the industry has been growing at twice the rate of the economy over the last decade. The 2005 UK Budget offered more support for the Creative Industries and the Scottish Arts Council set up Ideasmart (www.ideasmart.org/) to help more young people in the Creative Industries get their ideas into the workplace. Like every other sector, this sector has its hot spots in the UK. Current labour market intelligence which you can access through government websites can be very helpful. There will be significant increases in a demand for those at the higher skilled end of the work force, such as managers, professionals, associate professionals and those engaged in technical and service occupations.

Every sector has its hot spots and weak parts. Each region has its growing industries and those in decline. You can find out where your sector's hot spots are by looking at government websites relating to trade and industry, the economy and sites such as the UK Trade and Investment (www.invest.uktradeinvest.gov.uk/) but also in each of the Regional Development Agencies' (RDAs') websites. The RDAs in England have been created to ensure strong and sustainable economic growth and success, while ensuring quality of life and opportunity for those living in the area. They have their equivalents in Scotland, Wales and Northern Ireland. There are European RDAs too (www.eurada.gov). Look for labour market information at the regional and national level which will point you in the direction of the hot spots. In areas of traditional and declining industries, redundant skills and depleting resources, RDAs are responding by leading and creating initiatives in such areas by regenerating them, boosting learning opportunities and facilitating skill acquisition and start-ups. Cluster groups and localised graduate websites (see Further Information at the end of this book) may direct you to useful local networks.

Analyse the sector and size of company in it

The size of the niche area or sector will make a difference as to how competitive it is to get into. You may need to move abroad to get entry into your desired career or into an allied industry in your home country if that's where you want to stay.

Be aware of all the support available to you as a graduate and in the sector you wish to work in

As mentioned in the previous chapter, you need dig deep and search wide to find out what support is available in your area at these levels:

1   Business start-ups – your own.
2   Working in the creative industries – getting in and getting on.
3   Initiatives designed to strengthen the relationship between graduates and employers,
  ◆ in the SME market
  ◆ in the creative industries
  ◆ in any industry.

What initiatives are available to encourage employers to take on graduates?

Governments are investing a lot of money in developing skills and talent, and particularly so at the graduate end of the market. There are many initiatives, programmes, events, websites, help-lines, networking groups, advisory services and more to help you and your peers. In the UK, for example, RDAs are encouraging universities and businesses alike to retain skilled talent in their area and working to raise small companies' awareness of how graduates can benefit them. There is a strong connection between the skill levels in an area and the quality of working opportunities and lifestyle on offer which is why huge efforts are being made to regenerate those areas which are lagging behind. These bodies are also trying to encourage inward investment which should create more employment opportunities. Consider initiatives such as the Knowledge Transfer Partnerships (www.ktponline.org.uk) which enable graduates to undertake a project within a company while acquiring management training at the same time; and don't forget internships and work experience programmes (see www.work-experience.com). Graduates for Business is another programme which will give you the chance to gain that essential business experience while applying the skills from your course as you implement a project or product. Companies commission projects in a range of sectors. Many regional graduate careers service providers (see Useful Addresses at the end of this book) offer work placement programmes and schemes designed to boost your employability. This forms part of their drive to encourage graduates to remain in the area after their degree studies.

What support is available from local business or government groups?

Watch out for initiatives and support available. The names of these may change; some may be driven under the direction of one body one year (such as the Design Council in the UK) and then transferred over to another, perhaps a university, in the following year. Some may be targeted to areas in which strenuous efforts are being made to re-generate the economy.

Finding suitable employment opportunities

Employers use a range of methods to recruit employees and you should use a range of methods in your job hunting. Consider how employers recruit. They could enlist freelances or temps to save them taking on staff long term. But they also have a range of other options to them, including linking with schools, colleges and universities through careers fairs and presentations, their own websites or those of agencies, advertisements in the local press, looking at on-spec applications and finding students through work experience, internships and secondments. They could spread the net wider, hooking potential recruits in through agencies, the national press and specialist trade journals; some are even using radio and TV adverts. Many sites have vacancy listings, for example the British Design Innovation website has a Graduate Directory inviting employers to search for potential graduates (and students) in its disciplines.

Having identified where you want to work, search out those employers!

If you use a multitude of methods to find employers and seek the role you crave, you're more likely to land it. Stick to one or two, and you're going to have a harder trek. Walk into every circle shown in Figure 5.1 to hunt for the opportunities you're looking for and persist in your efforts until you find success.

In addition, you should:

1   run a search for all the relevant employers using all the means at your disposal, including Kompass and Dun and Bradstreet, both excellent online resources of buisness and company information;

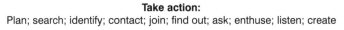

Take action:
Plan; search; identify; contact; join; find out; ask; enthuse; listen; create

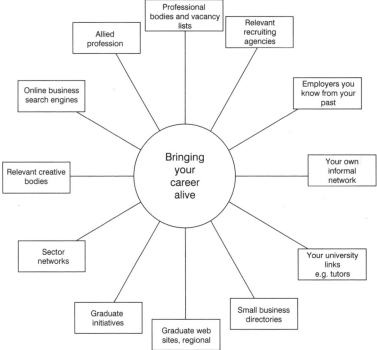

Figure 5.1

2 use your local library which should have sector reports, books and information about the local area, trade and national magazines, phone and trade directories;

3 register for any email alerts with online agencies to pick up new jobs which come in that might interest you.

Hint: You can do a search for businesses at http://local.google. com/. Use several search terms to maximise the effectiveness of your search.

Go on the alert for vacancies

Of course you can register your details with various online agencies, associations and groups, which have the facility to enable employers to search out someone with the skills and talents they need. This does work, and also gives you the opportunity to receive email alerts when new jobs come in and to browse the vacancies available and make contact with the appropriate agency or employer.

Online and printed directories can help you identify small and medium-sized companies. An example is www.creative-london.co.uk, a directory of small companies active in architecture, advertising, art and antiques, crafts, design, electronic publishing, fashion, film and video, games software, music, publishing, performing arts and TV and radio. The Producers Alliance for Cinema and Television at www.pact.co.uk is the trade association in the UK representing independent television, feature film, animation and interactive media production companies. There's also Shooting People which enables you to get in touch with others working in the independent film industry at www.shootingpeople.org and www.broadcastfreelancer. com which you can register with for a fee and which gives you access to hundreds of jobs with daily alerts and lots of great links and careers information. By registering your details, employers can find you. Keep your personal details up-to-date, so that they reflect any extra experience and skills you've acquired.

Going through recruitment companies

Recruitment agencies are selected by employers to find recruits for them. Many employers have long-standing relationships with agencies, so agency consultants build up an extensive knowledge of what the employer is like to work for and what sort of career path candidates can expect upon successful application and starting.

Agencies offer various services to their candidates, including help with CVs (although some agencies have their own particular CV format to send to clients) and profiling so that you can work out what sort of work would suit you best. Your consultant should have a clear idea of trends in the sector and how your career will fit into it, and he or she should enjoy strong links with the industry. Many offer training, and some run networking evenings. It's essential to remember that your consultant is human, too, so treat him or her as you would like to be treated.

Online recruitment has become big business. Many online agencies and professional bodies offer the facility of receiving email alerts, enabling you to receive notice that new (relevant) vacancies are available. Newspapers and trade magazines also have online vacancy boards and often send newsletters. You may also be able to post your CV on some sites for potential employers to view.

If you want to get into a specific industry, look for agencies which are active in and focus on it, with a good track record – they are more likely to have a strong network and an ear to the ground for opportunities.

You can quickly access a huge number of agencies in specific sectors by visiting http://www.agencycentral.co.uk which has agencies listed under sector and also has a full list of agencies offering graduate positions.

Go to where the action is, ready to sell your talents and creativity

This includes careers events and trade fairs, not just those surrounding the area of employment and shows such as New Designers, and the large design shows but anywhere you are likely to find companies involved in the business. Many of these will have demonstrations, workshops, seminars on starting your own business and marketing your own work, selling yourself, promoting your wares on the web and building good client relationships. Many events will provide a forum for you to get out there, meet and greet and hand people your business card. You can find a list of the larger shows at www.biztradeshows.com where you can find details by industry or country, including Fabrics and Textiles, Home Textiles, Leather,

Architecture and Designing, Apparel and Clothing. There's also www.eventseye.com, another global listing of events by location, topic or date. Check too your local business network sites because they also may list sector specific events and exhibitions. In the UK, www.exhibitions.co.uk has details of craft, music, clothing, textile and footwear, home, lifestyle and giftware. If you're planning to go as an exhibitor, www.businesslink.gov.uk has some first-class tips on how to make the most of a show. The website www.creative.fastchannel.com has details of events in the film and television industry.

Plan for a successful event

When you approach stand-holders, an introductory chat about their company and what it's developing and working on can quickly lead to a sentence or two about yourself and your career goals. Regardless of whether you're going to a trade show or careers event, tips for a successful show include:

- Pre-register online to avoid lengthy queues.
- Identify the people you want to meet and visit their websites *before* you go. On arrival, visit their stands *first* while you're fresh and full of energy.
- Create a business card to hand out. Put your contact details (email and mobile number) and your most recent or relevant educational qualification on one side with niche areas; and the sort of company you're looking to work for, plus skills you have to contribute on the other.
- Prepare questions to ask before you go to avoid mumbling and stumbling over awkward introductory waffle. *'What advice do you have for someone in my position?'* and *'What job hunting strategies can you suggest I use?'* can be two helpful questions to get insider information and give you other routes to follow.
- Ask open questions. *'Do you recruit graduates of any discipline?'* is a closed question requiring a simple yes or no answer; you won't learn much. *'What degrees do you particularly look to recruit?'* is hard to answer with a yes or no. As an open question, it gives you more information and enables you to engage the person you're talking to in further conversation.

- Don't start off by asking *'What can your company do for me?'* or *'What can your company offer me?'* Promote yourself as someone who has a lot to contribute to the right employer.
- If someone looks busy, wait until they are quieter.
- Talk to people in the café areas. Make some small talk about the fair – *'What a great opportunity to meet people!' 'What a great venue!' 'Isn't it good to sit down?' 'Are you here as an exhibitor?' 'What does your company do?' 'I'll stop by and see you at your stand!' 'Could I contact you next week and ask for some of your time?'* Smaller companies may not have a stand, but you might bump into a representative from one if you start talking to people in the café areas.
- If you get stuck talking to people who are being negative about your general situation, *'There are too many of us graduating!'* politely say goodbye and wish them luck and walk away. Focus on what you *do* want and ways to increase your chances of succeeding in getting it. Sitting and moping isn't one of them.
- When the event is over, walk away and reflect over what you've learnt about the opportunities available and yourself. Bring together action points and carry them through. Business cards create dust if unused; you want them to create results.
- Write and thank the people you met at the show by email or letter. If you have a web CV, you can attach the address under your contact details at the bottom. After the event, identify those people you need to follow up and contact them.

Heading to other shores – working abroad

This may be appropriate if you're thinking, *'Well, my industry is dead in this country. So what now?'* In this case, you have a number of choices before you. You can switch to an allied industry, in which your degree may still come in useful, or you can change altogether, or start your own business. Could you, for example, export anything which is needed by the industry in those regions where it is flourishing? This could be easier said than you think, thanks to the Internet. Find out more from the Institute of Export. And, of course, you could consider: *'Where else is it functioning? How might it use my skills? Should I head out there for a holiday and see what's happening and whether there might be anything for me in that region?'* If you choose to stay put, hard though this sounds, there is no point in whining about it because such an action won't change anything (which is why it will be all the more frustrating). Consider alternatives.

Questions to ask include:

1 What is the local job market like?
2 How do employers recruit staff there? What is involved in the recruitment process?
3 How should I write a CV for that country? What should I include?
4 What organisations and websites can I turn to for advice and information (e.g. Prospects and Hobsons)?
5 Does my professional body or trade organisation have any relevant links in the country I wish to work in? What support can it give me?
6 How will my current qualifications transfer? Will they be accepted? Many professional bodies are working with other countries across borders to ensure the smooth transfer and recognition of qualifications from one nation to another. Are these countries more interested in experience?
7 How does the working environment differ? What is acceptable behaviour and what is not?
8 What level of job would I have with the competences I have got?
9 Will I need to take additional tests to prove my competence in my new country before I can start work
10 Where in the world will my knowledge and skills be needed in the future?

Put *willing to re-locate* on your CV or business card but be prepared to actually do it. If you're focusing in on one country and you satisfy visa requirements, say so on your CV or covering letter (see www.workpermit.com). Look out for events and newspaper supplements promoting life or companies abroad. Use your network to help you get work overseas, read journals and newspapers and make use of embassies and state employment services such as http://europa.eu.int/eures. The European Job Mobility Portal is one of the places where European candidates can see an employer's vacancy and employers can multi-search for CVs which may meet their needs. It links the public employment services in Europe and helps people take up work in other member states of the EEA. It has lots of information on jobs, learning, labour markets, health, registering for work when you arrive and working conditions.

You could also sign up with a recruitment agency that has international offices or connections, or go through an organisation offering placements abroad, such as GAP, or simply do it yourself. Don't forget to tap into any twinning arrangements and Chamber of Commerce organisations (www.chamberonline.co.uk/). These have links to trade organisations and research they've undertaken into markets abroad. Their site has details of all the UK Chambers, overseas Chambers in the UK, British Chambers of Commerce overseas and the Council of British Chambers of Commerce in Continental Europe. It also has an excellent export zone and business services on offer.

Returning home later on

The various locations you choose to work need to be kept in mind when you're considering where to settle later in life. Sooner or later, you may want to return home. Watch for any trends or new laws or regulations there which may impede on your ability to return when the time comes. Consider the financial implications for your future. How will working abroad affect any pension due to you later in life, for example, be it state or private? Read *Working Abroad: The Complete Guide to Overseas Employment* by Jonathan Reuvid (see Further Reading at the end of this book).

Your next steps

1   List employers in the sector you wish to work and to research in the country you want to work in.

2   Develop a short list by researching them. Continue your research through the Internet, careers fairs, finding out about their products and services through your network and news items.

3   Who do you know, or which sector networks could you tap into, to acquire an introduction to these companies? At this point, your networking efforts will really pay off.

Why not go to places where graduates *don't* normally look for work to stand out from the crowd? While all your peers are heading for the same avenues, do what they wouldn't think of doing. While they are all gunning for the big corporates, what could you do to steer your own course that nobody else would think of doing? When you come across a company which really excites you, consider the people who work for it behind the scenes and at its frontage. Why shouldn't you join them?

Moving things forward ... do you, don't you?

Find out more about the organisation and its career opportunities, but don't confine your research to the company's website. Delve further and wider for any mention of it in the local, national or international media. Most employers try to provide as much information as they can about their organisation to job hunters so that the latter can ensure they are applying to the right sort of company for them. Why not see if you can get in touch with someone appropriate at the company to see if you can visit and look around, and talk about the opportunities available?

Questions to ask of a potential employer

1   What is its mission and what does it want to do and achieve? Does it excite you?

2   What messages does it give you about its values and what it deems to be important? What values does the organisation or company portray in its advertising, literature, image and brand? Look for evidence that it upholds these values. Do they excite you?

3   What is the size of the organisation and how will that impact on the way people work and the opportunities within it? What does it say about how to apply for work?

4   Where is it located? Is it spread over a number of sites?

5   What is the structure and hierarchy; is there just the one company or are there a number of subsidiary companies within one group?

6   How is it organised? A small company may have one person looking after IT, marketing, sales, web design and HR which would put a generalist business degree to excellent use; a large one will have a department of people for each of these elements enabling you to focus on one area.

7   What is the company's is financial position? If it is not healthy, your career there may be short. What are its strengths, weaknesses, opportunities and threats?

8   What sort of people work for it? Look at employee profiles. What do they get involved with outside of work? How do they describe themselves, the company and their roles?

Find out what the company is doing to be innovative and competitive. Where does it see itself going and what is its place in the market? If there is no evidence of such activities, ask yourself whether the company will exist in five years' time? Can you contribute to the company's overall business development and expansion? Careful research into its finances and diplomatic questioning at interview time can help you assess such a state.

Nine key questions to ask yourself

1   What could you contribute to this organisation in terms of skills and qualities?
2   Is this the sort of place you'd look forward to walking into every Monday morning?
3   Could you see yourself working for them in five years' time?
4   Can they offer you the future you're looking for?
5   What would you need to do to make the career progress you want to enjoy? What support would you get from the company?
6   What is the organisation's view on work–life balance? What specific examples are there to support this view?
7   How could you secure a foot in the door?
8   Is there a vacancy right now you could apply for or will you need to make contact on spec?
9   What actions are you going to take next and when?

You could multiply the opportunities before you if you consider working for an organisation short term, perhaps on a contract basis – plenty of professionals do – to get experience and get your foot in the door. Part-time work will leave you free to job hunt for the role you really want, or to develop your own business while bringing some money in. A small company may not have enough work to warrant taking someone on full time but it may offer you part-time work. Think laterally and creatively when you're job hunting.

Starting your own business

There is more help around than ever before for those with an entrepreneurial spirit but still too many start-ups fail for lack of sufficient advice and research. The BusinessLink network in England helps small companies and start-ups. Visit www.businesslink.gov.uk to find your local link. There's information on setting up a business, writing a business plan, accessing funding, growing your business and even selling it on. There are also links to the sister organisations in Scotland, Wales and Northern Ireland.

Consider initiatives

Aside from Flying Start (see page 36), other national examples of organisations helping people to set up on their own include Shell LiveWIRE, the Prince's Trust, Start-ups and the Prime Initiative for the over 50s (see Useful Addresses at the end of this book). Some initiatives may be national in nature, others very local.

As an example, the National Endowment for Science, Technology and the Arts (NESTA) announced a scheme to support graduates to build new types of companies and business markets. Its Creative Pioneer Programme will support a number of individuals every year who have graduated within the last three years. They take a three-week course at the Academy, and come face-to-face with creative entrepreneurs who know what it's like to set up a business. Up to 25 of the attendees will win Pioneer Awards of up to £35,000 to start their own business together with on-going support from a mentor (www.nesta.org.uk/academy).

The Sew-East programme (www.emep.co.uk and look for the Sew-East page link) provides information, advice and funding (to which conditions apply) to new and existing businesses in the fashion sector in the east of London. It offers one-to-one specialist advice, business awareness seminars and workshops which are related to the industry, specialist networking events and workshops, links to manufacturers and designers and access to finance. Why not check into the Creative Industries sector in your region to find out what's on offer?

Eight questions to consider

1 What's your vision and what do you want to achieve with this business?
2 What are your products and services?

3   What to you need to get up and running, e.g.:
  ◆ somewhere to work from;
  ◆ equipment needed to set up (you may have a lot of this
    already);
  ◆ computer/lap top;
  ◆ communications – Internet, phone, fax;
  ◆ marketing and publicity materials – possibly a website,
    business cards, brochures, membership of professional and
    business networks;
  ◆ insurance, professional indemnity and public liability;
  ◆ training;
  ◆ a salary/wage?
4   Who can support you?
5   What new skills and knowledge will you need?
6   Who are your competitors?
7   What research do you need to do?
8   Where will you get funding from?

Be alert to opportunity

Watch the world carefully and keep up-to-date with events and
trends. Are there any booming economies which would benefit from
your skills and talents? Events which can be disastrous for some people provide huge opportunities for others. For example, a company
makes 500 people redundant; that's unfortunate for the 500, but a
great business opportunity for careers coaches and redundancy advisers. Similarly, the Olympics in Beijing in 2008 and in London in
2012 will offer great opportunities for people with the right skills.

Summary action points

  Move your thinking further forward:
1   What are agencies in the region doing to encourage businesses
    to take on graduates, particularly those in my sector?
2   How much do I know about the work I want to do and how
    to get 'in' to it?
3   Where are most of the employers located in this sector?
4   Which other areas are showing a rapid growth?
5   What am I doing to enjoy life and have time out while I'm
    working towards my goals?

Chapter 6

Proving yourself
From scholar to worker

One minute you're a student and the next you're not. You may choose to have some time out or get going on your career straightaway, but whichever path you take, there's a big difference between the two. The earlier you start preparing for life after your university days, the easier it will be to settle in work and life afterwards.

Making the psychological switch

There is quite a switch from being a student to becoming an employee or self-employed, because the impact of your work and how well you do it affects other people, as shown in Table 6.1.

The 'learning to do' referred to above relates to those things you cannot be taught until you start work, such as product knowledge specific to the organisation you join. But at the very least, employers want to know that you know how to behave at work and that you understand what work is like.

At work, you'll still get the person who does it all at the last minute, those who are indecisive, bullies, patronising or negative, who spout 'We've always done it like this', and see no reason to change. There are the moody, sulky and lazy, working alongside power-crazy, highly competitive workaholics and you'll need to deal with them all. Your skills and talents in motivating and managing people will be well tested as you progress, and work to bring out the best in your team. You'll need your influencing and persuading skills to encourage those around you to see the benefits of what you want to do. But your experiences at university will have given you a good start in speaking up for yourself and getting along with people from all different backgrounds and with their own aspirations. Add work experience in a real live work situation, and you can put the above skills into place and make the psychological switch.

Table 6.1

As a student		As an employee
Studying	and	Working
Being a student	and	an employee/employer
Learning	and	Doing or learning to do ...
Student responsibilities	and	Responsibilities at work towards: team; clients, customers; company/employer; your own colleagues, peers
The hours you choose to work	and	The hours you're expected to work
Holidays	and	Average 4 weeks holiday – in the US, probably 1 or 2 weeks in the first few years
The way you dress and behave	and	The image and behaviour that's right and appropriate for work
Long-term personal goals	and	Vision, mission, targets need the goodwill and motivation of everyone on board
Rules and regulations in your university	and	Employment laws, health and safety, professional regulations
Meeting deadlines – it's just you that suffers	and	Meeting deadlines – other people are depending on you
The pace of life – you can dictate it	and	The pace of work is dictated by the industry and demands of clients and customers. Your day can change dramatically on receipt of a phone call. People expect fast responses. Are you adaptable and flexible?
Your performance – it affects just you	and	Your performance can affect that of your team and the company – it can clinch a deal, save the company money
You can control pretty much most things in your life	and	There are many things you can control but equally there are many you cannot

Transferable skills are essential to enjoy life and excel at work

List everything you've done during your university days and you will be astonished at what you've achieved formally and informally. To do it all, you will have used skills which transfer from one aspect of life to another, such as communication. To communicate effectively with clients and colleagues, family and friends, you need to express yourself clearly, orally and in writing through email, letter and fax. You need to be able to empathise with and understand the needs of others. As a designer, for example, you will need to take a brief from a client, to redefine it and understand you have the scope of the matter to hand, and then come up with a solution for the client. You're solving their problem for them.

Rank the transferable skills in Figure 6.1 in order of your strength, 5 being the strongest.

Now find evidence for each one looking through your list of extra-curricular activities, voluntary efforts, work experience and

	5	4	3	2	1
Organising/planning					
Communicating, orally					
Communicating, written					
Learning					
Creativity					
Decision making					
Self-motivation					
Strategic planning					
Handling change					
Problem solving					
Team working					
Leadership					
Adaptability, flexibility					
Self-awareness					
Commercial awareness					

Figure 6.1

academic work. Which are your strengths? Which are your weaknesses and how are you tackling those? Take each transferable skill and give an example of a time when you've used it. Consider all the angles you might be asked about it.

Have you made the most of university life?

University days offer the chance to create a life out of a blank canvas. Employers will be looking to see how you occupied your time and what you learnt from your activities. They'll be looking for evidence of your passion for your subject, such as any shows you've been to and competitions you've entered. Also, what projects have you done over and above your coursework? What were the modes of learning you used which could transfer over to the workplace, such as giving presentations, undertaking research, debating a point in seminars and tutorials, critiquing your work, taking an idea from conception to fruition, working in a team to solve a problem?

Effectiveness and high performance at work is built on the right attitude, a professional competence and approach, product and sector knowledge, a *drive* to make things happen and soft skills. At university, you develop skills through various academic and extra-curricular activities. To progress your career, you need continued exposure to different experiences and the right training and personal development, all of which continue to expand your capabilities, push back your comfort zones and build on your soft or transferable skills. Self-awareness, self-promotion and self-presentation also count, along with keeping abreast of career developments and news in your field. Figure 6.2 shows how university and work link together incorporating all these elements.

This extends beyond work!

Throughout your life, both in and out of work, you'll need to manage a number of ingredients, as shown in Table 6.2.

Who are you?

This is not just about your qualifications and experience to date. They certainly contribute and play a part, but this is more about how you arrived at the whole-rounded individual you are now. It's not about *'Well, I completed my UCAS form and made my six choices,*

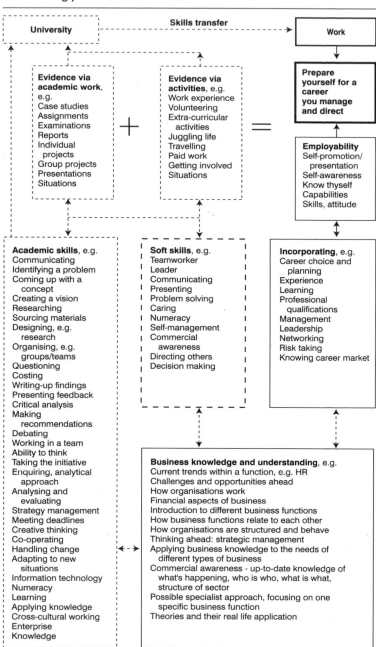

University — Skills transfer → **Work**

Evidence via academic work, e.g.
Case studies
Assignments
Examinations
Reports
Individual projects
Group projects
Presentations
Situations

+

Evidence via activities, e.g.
Work experience
Volunteering
Extra-curricular activities
Juggling life
Travelling
Paid work
Getting involved
Situations

=

Prepare yourself for a career you manage and direct

Employability
Self-promotion/presentation
Self-awareness
Know thyself
Capabilities
Skills, attitude

Academic skills, e.g.
Communicating
Identifying a problem
Coming up with a concept
Creating a vision
Researching
Sourcing materials
Designing, e.g. research
Organising, e.g. groups/teams
Questioning
Costing
Writing-up findings
Presenting feedback
Critical analysis
Making recommendations
Debating
Working in a team
Ability to think
Taking the initiative
Enquiring, analytical approach
Analysing and evaluating
Strategy management
Meeting deadlines
Creative thinking
Co-operating
Handling change
Adapting to new situations
Information technology
Numeracy
Learning
Applying knowledge
Cross-cultural working
Enterprise
Knowledge

Soft skills, e.g.
Teamworker
Leader
Communicating
Presenting
Problem solving
Caring
Numeracy
Self-management
Commercial awareness
Directing others
Decision making

Incorporating, e.g.
Career choice and planning
Experience
Learning
Professional qualifications
Management
Leadership
Networking
Risk taking
Knowing career market

Business knowledge and understanding, e.g.
Current trends within a function, e.g. HR
Challenges and opportunities ahead
How organisations work
Financial aspects of business
Introduction to different business functions
How business functions relate to each other
How organisations are structured and behave
Thinking ahead: strategic management
Applying business knowledge to the needs of different types of business
Commercial awareness - up-to-date knowledge of what's happening, who is who, what is what, structure of sector
Possible specialist approach, focusing on one specific business function
Theories and their real life application

Figure 6.2

Table 6.2

Yourself	Information technology
People	Resources
Teams	Materials
Time	Projects
Money	Deadlines
Your energy	Research
The client's expectations	The facilities around you
Your future	Your suppliers

and then sat and prayed that I'd get in to my first choice!' It's about, how did you come to apply at all? What and who moulded your decisions and what did you need *within yourself* to get to where you are today? What resources did you pull out of your body, heart, mind and soul to make your degree happen and how can you build on them and use them to maximum effect throughout your life? Who did you work alongside as you strove to achieve your mutual goals? *(That's teamwork!)*

It's also about your values, and what matters to you. After all, you must have chosen the path you took for a reason. So what lies behind and within you, what makes you tick, what drives, inspires and motivates you. What challenges and dramas have you faced? How have you tackled them? *(That's problem solving.)* If you wrote your life story, what particular achievements would you want your readers to know about? What journeys would you want to tell them about? How can you show them that you've turned your plans into action? Have you done a stint of travelling, or juggled study and work at the same time? *(Shows adaptability and flexibility, planning and organisation.)* When have you really had to knuckle down and make things happen? Were there times when you kept going when everything else seems to be going against you? How many times have you failed at something – anything – and you've tried and tried again until success came your way? *(Persistence, motivation, drive, resilience.)* What changes have you dealt with in your life; if you've driven them yourself how have you tapped into your drive and energy and passion to make them happen? If they happened outside your control, how did you handle them? *(Resilience, ability to cope with change.)* What negative experiences have you been through that you've learnt from? How could you show a stranger the person you truly are, as opposed to a bunch of qualifications listed neatly on a page? *(That's written communication, persuading, influencing, expressing.)* What sort of person would they see? It's these qualities that you need to bring out in your CV or interviews when applying for jobs or courses. *(That's self-promotion.)*

It's also about those things which prompted you to make the choices you have in work, play and leisure, and in the friends you hang around with. *(That shows what motivates you.)* What circumstances have you grown up in which have influenced you, your actions, your choices and the messages you've taken on board about yourself, life and the opportunities ahead? *(Decision making and action planning skills here.)* What have you done to challenge them? *(You don't settle for just anything and the status quo!)* What have you done to help yourself? These sorts of things have all contributed to make up the person you are by influencing and moulding you over the years. It will also show you that being successful – however you define success – takes tremendous hard graft, self-discipline and continual, sustained effort. Without ingredients such as these, success all too often feels hollow, empty and unsatisfying. Look at all the times you've been proactive and what the results were. Look at the opportunities you created for yourself by getting off your backside and making something happen. *(Taking the initiative.)* If you want to be successful in the way you envisage success, you need to do that again and again.

It's also about your professional and personal development as an artist or designer, and how you untapped your creativity. Who or what has inspired you along the way? Can you discuss and debate the various merits of those key people working in the niche sector you want to get into, those from whom you've taken inspiration and courage? How do you tend to get your ideas and what happens from then on in? How can you show that you've worked with a team of people to bring an idea to fruition? Where do you pull your ideas from and how do you research an idea and the process along the way?

However, you've studied towards your degree, be it full time, part time or by distance learning, so congratulate yourself. Go out with a group of friends and sink a few drinks. But take time to quietly, independently and proudly assess what you've achieved and, crucially, the characteristics in your personality, the motivators and drivers which have empowered you to success, such as persistence, determination and curiosity. You've had the endurance to get through a degree and developed the ability to network, form working relationships fast, to take responsibility for your own career development and learning and to be resourceful.

Acknowledge your strengths and resources in writing

Written down, they will give you a lift, especially if you're feeling low. Whatever stage of life you're at, you'll need to draw on all your resources to create the future you want. Get ready to dig deep and raise your energy levels, standards, focus, persistence and drive to a higher level to propel yourself into making it happen. Finally, you'll be able to tell employers more succinctly what lies behind the person you are – and the person you want to be, thereby selling yourself more effectively. Self-presentation and promotion is an important skill at work today.

The power of work experience

Work experience strengthens your hand in the employment market, particularly if it is targeted towards the career you intend to follow and structured in such a way that you can learn and put the theory you have learnt on your degree course into practice. Employers can see you in action for themselves: the way you walk and talk, think and act, behave and motivate, initiate and inspire, work and apply your new-found knowledge. They want to see how effective you are and how you achieve results. In fact, employers rate work experience and internships as a highly effective way to find graduate recruits. There are many schemes on offer throughout the year for varying periods of time. Their entry is often highly competitive, requiring the same professional approach and strategy to achieve success as job hunting.

The small and medium enterprise (SME) market in its own right can give you the chance to put your foot in the door. There may be a scheme running in your area to help companies and graduates benefit each other. The National Council for Work Experience has a lot more information on its website (www.work-experience.org). Look for opportunities to gain experience through professional bodies and trade associations' websites too. Check out www.step.org.uk which arranges placements with companies for a year or shorter periods of time. Many of the websites listed in this book have details of work placements, internships and residencies and you need to get to know which sites are most suitable for you. Internships and work experience placements are very competitive and it can be hard to survive for three months with just your travel expenses. However, it is an excellent way in, so consider it as an investment, just as your university studies are.

You don't have to sign up for a specific scheme to get experience. You could approach a company directly, which may be a great way to get into a smaller company that may not be aware of opportunities to join placement schemes. Keep trying and persisting.

1 Identify what it is that you need to practise at work – are there particular skills you want to use?
2 Pinpoint what you will bring to the employer – enthusiasm and a passion for what you're doing are a start.
3 Give the employer examples of what you can do and what you would like to do, so that he has a menu of choices.
4 Show him what you have done so far, so that he has a clear idea of what you're capable of.
5 Give an allotted timescale but be flexible.
6 Find out if the company has a project which needs to be done which no-one else has time to do.
7 Ask for an assessment of your work at the end, so that the employer can write a testimonial and you can together work out what you have achieved and got out of the placement.

Work experience should play a central role in your sales strategy when you start job hunting. It shows that you know what you're letting yourself in for. You can talk about your experiences and achievements at interview and demonstrate your effectiveness through the job-specific and transferable skills you've used. You can prove how you can be relied on to get results, to make things happen and to achieve. You can prove your passion for, and belief in, what you're doing and that you've got your hands dirty. You can talk the lingo, understand the frustrations, challenges, issues, opportunities and threats. As a rule, the longer and more relevant the experience, the more beneficial it will be.

If you've found a work experience on your own, turn it into a constructive learning time. Identify what you want out of it and what you have to offer before you approach an employer. Find out if there is a project you can do to practise specific skills and put your course theory into practice. Observe closely and ask the right questions and you'll acquire an insight into how the different parts of the organisation pull together as everyone works to fulfil the mission or vision set out in its profile.

You can pick up the language relevant to the sector and the organisation or company itself. You can pick up business lingo relevant to the business world with terms such as 'profit and loss', 'added value', 'key performance indicators', and you'll understand what they are. Listening skills are important if you're to pick up the language and way of working specific to the business. Each one has its own terminology relating to its systems, protocol, meetings, hierarchy, and many have their own intranet. Work experience gives you an insight into how companies function and helps you make those all-important contacts. *'I've got a friend who works in PR. Shall I mention you to her? She could give you a call for a chat.'*

Finally, remember that working at the bottom of the organisation is a great way to learn how the various parts work, who the key decision makers are and why the bottom line is so important.

Work to close any skills gaps

Every industry has its problems recruiting staff with the right skills. In many niche areas, there are cluster groups, forums and groups of employers, industry specialists and training providers who are trying to tackle the problem and encourage employers to offer (graduates) a way in and a structured learning environment. Ideas which are being developed include apprenticeship programmes, business realisation schemes, training programmes and career-entry initiatives. Go to the heart of the industry to find out what is being undertaken in yours. Skillset (www.skillset.org) for the audio visual industries has great examples of such initiatives.

Meantime, why not show someone who works in the sector a copy of your CV and ask them where your skills gaps are? How can you go about closing them? It may be that a short training programme will do the trick, or perhaps a stint of work experience with exposure to a particular area will help.

What behaviours and practices do you need to elicit to make your 'it' happen?

* Be very determined. Push for your corner, but remain polite.
* Get focused.
* Be prepared to sacrifice something else in your life so that you can give what you really want the hours it deserves. True

friends will understand if you can only meet them once a fort-night or once a week.

Go out there and start building up your portfolio

1   Start acquiring clients. Ask them for feedback on how you handled them and their business, from acquiring a commission, to discussing pricing, invoicing and their pleasure and satisfaction with the end product. How much leeway do you have while studying to produce items and designs you can then sell commercially? What facilities can you use at your university to help you, during term time and the holidays?

2   While you're looking for clients, build up a portfolio by doing things for yourself, for example working on projects in the area you want to get into. Examples could be designing jewellery, furniture or coming up with a perfect design campaign for that health food shop on the high street. Can you and some of your fellow students find outlets to sell these to?

3   Use your network, formal and informal, to promote your products and services so that people know what you're doing. It just needs one person to mention it in the right place at the right time.

4   Get your work out there where it can be seen, at shows, exhibitions, trade events, student presentations and in the press. If you don't plan to exhibit, you can at least attend.

5   Hundreds of small local charities struggle on without the support and back-up of a large organisation. Find out if a local charity has a project it needs doing but doesn't have the resources to do it and needs your skills and talents. Visit www. designfortheworld.org or www.do-it.org for more ideas.

6   Look for a problem in society and find a way to solve it through designing a product. Why not approach the task with another graduate whose skills complement yours?

7   Offer to do some work for a heavily discounted rate in return for a testimonial to put on your marketing literature or website.

Take part in competitions, exhibitions, awards and collections

The D&AD Student Awards (www.dandad.org/studentawards06), for example, are a terrific way to get exposure in front of industry experts. Advertising, environmental design, integrated communication, graphic design, illustration, brand identity and product design and innovation are just some of the briefs. In 2005, students from 32 countries entered. Winning work is shown both online and offline in the D&AD Student Annual and in 2005, 3,000 of these were sent to international advertising and design businesses.

The New Designers Show is another opportunity for you to show off your designs and wares (www.newdesigners.com). In 2005, just under half of all exhibitors came away with commissions, work offers and work placements. Many shows have seminars to help you with your career, with advice and information on setting up on your own, marketing your work, making contacts, keeping everything legal, the way you can structure your business and lots more.

Draw up a year and month planner

1   Undertake a complete search of all the shows, exhibitions, awards and competitions you wish to enter as an exhibitor (which will mean preparing something to display) or attend as a walk-in visitor (which will mean identifying what you want to get out of the visit prior to the event). Put them on a wall planner, along with any other known commitments such as deadlines for course assignments, projects, job application deadlines, exams, your graduation day, key social and family dates, and anything else which comes to mind.

2   Of those shows you plan to attend as an exhibitor, if this is your first show, how much information can you glean from the show organisers and the material they send out about the event? Many events have a list of exhibitors up on their websites prior to the show, enabling you to make contact with exhibitors you'd like to meet to arrange a chat during the show. Why not contact some of the people who attended as exhibitors last year to see what advice they have for you as a new entrant? Can you arrange to meet them there for a coffee to ask their advice if they'll be there or use the event as a way to secure an introduction to ask for help?

3   Plan how long it will take to prepare for the events if you're going to exhibit at them. If you are unsure, ask a more experienced designer or artist. What exactly do you need to do to put on the best showing you can? Apart from any products and designs, this may include preparing marketing material about yourself, such as your CV (up-to-date), a business card, a CD showing your work and giving CV details, and even a website you can refer people to.

4   How important is each event to you and your career? What else is likely to be featuring in your life at the time and in the weeks ahead which may be competing for your time, energy and attention? How can you organise yourself so that you really are at your best for what is most important to you? Can you talk to those important to you in your life to ask for their particular support and understanding in the weeks leading up to the event?

5   What exactly do you want from each show – Contacts? Work? Commissions? Who else will be there that you could make sure you make contact with? What price will you be charging (roughly) for any commissions you get? Who can help you with this advice – Tutors? Professional bodies? Are you prepared to handle any approaches made to you for your work from a mental, practical and business point of view?

6   Allow time after the event to follow through any work you need to do, such as following up contacts and handling requests for information about you and your work, capitalising on any positives such as wins or offers of work. Can you send an article back to your home town newspaper, for example *'Local Student Wins Art Award!'* or go on a local radio show? Local press like to hear about students from their area doing well; you'll find details and contacts from the Newspaper Society at www.newspapersoc.org.uk/ or worldwide at http://www.wrx.zen.co.uk.

Start behaving and immersing yourself in the field you want to be in

If you're job hunting, devote full-time effort to the task. Keep your ambitions and goals at the forefront of your mind, or they will lose their prominence in your heart and it will take more effort to make them happen, especially if you consider yourself to be in a 'lower 'level' role right now. Position yourself to get out of it, either by moving or staying put, or one of two things can happen, as shown in Figure 6.3.

Network, network, network

Take the wheel of networking in Figure 6.4. At some time in your life, you may focus on one segment more than others; you may want to add or delete a segment. Aim for a balanced wheel, so that you can tap into the support you need for a healthy, balanced life and successful, happy career. Tap into every corner to see if any (albeit unexpectedly) can provide you with the opportunity you need to truly kick off your career and life in the direction you want it to go.

1   What are you doing to make something happen in each segment to create the career and life you want?

2   Which do you need to focus on *more* to get the results you need and make the connections you want?

3   Which section(s) should the *hub* of your network be at right now so that you can tackle the most important and urgent issues in your life?

4   How much activity do you have in it or them at the moment? How much time are you spending on accessing them and getting yourself known? How often are you making new contacts in it? Which is yielding the best results?

5   What do you need to do to make sure the sector you need to have the strongest network in is up to par to get the results you need in your life?

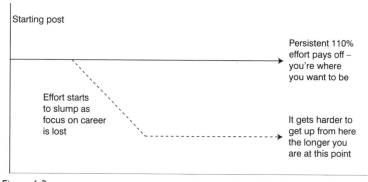

Figure 6.3

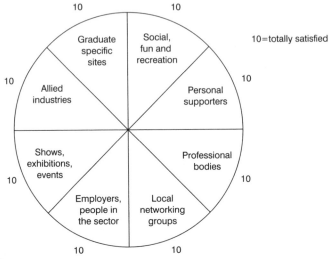

Figure 6.4

Prepare your portfolio

Make sure your portfolio is ready to show to potential employers. It should be easy to carry, be waterproof and sealed for safety to prevent your work falling out. It should also tell the story about your creative history; how you have developed your work and craft, what and who has influenced you along the way. View it as a creative CV, a marketing tool, a showpiece and be proud of it. Put in a variety of your work, using different layouts, pages, colour, detail, size, textures and detail so that it shows your creativity off on its own. Organise it in such a way that you feel comfortable talking people through it and you can find things easily. Put your more recent work towards the front. You may need to take samples out for a couple of interviewers to pass round, so keep the contents loose.

Be prepared to talk people through your portfolio. Give an introductory couple of sentences with regards to each piece – what the idea was behind it, how you approached it, what materials you used, etc. and then consider it in hindsight. Evaluate your own work from a stand-back point of view and take any feedback from those who you're discussing your work with calmly and objectively. Talk people through it, just as you would talk clients through a design you've created for them.

Showing off your work

Create a CD which is easy to navigate and which holds details of your work on it, together with a brief description surrounding each piece. Include your contact details and a CV. Keep adding to it, so that you have regular new pieces of work to show off and discuss.

Prepare to present your portfolio

Make sure it is professionally presented with your most recent work first, and include working drawings, details, visuals, presentation drawings and finished photos. Prepare to describe how you worked through a project from idea and conception to finish. Offer opportunities to ask questions. Take your most recent sketch book along so that you can show how you kick ideas for new concepts around. Show that you are keeping your skills and ideas alive.

Temping your way to a career

Like work experience, temping gives you the opportunity to show what you can do and will often lead to a permanent role.

Five steps to getting 'in' to a company through a temping

1   Hook up with a specialist agency which focuses on the specific sector you want to work in. If you're still thinking about what you want to do, sign up with a high street name which covers many sectors to broaden your insight and experience. A visit to the company's website will help you assess its strengths and focus and track record.

2   When you sign up with an agency, dress as if you're going for an interview so that the agency knows it can send you out with confidence. Your consultant should talk through your skills, competencies and career goals. Ask how often and by what method you should keep in touch. Check emails and your mobile regularly for messages. Try to get two, three-week or month assignments together in one sector to enhance your CV's consistency. Be more flexible at first and show you can be trusted first before you get choosey.

3   Look for ways to put the knowledge and skills you've acquired through your university experience into practice in the company you're with. Ask the company for projects or you can do them voluntarily to help develop your skills. Reflect weekly on skills and knowledge you're acquiring. Which environments have you thrived most in? What have you achieved? Get feedback from your agency and the company you're with.

4   Update your CV regularly and ensure the agency has a copy so that they can send out your most recent one. Focus on your transferable skills and consider exactly how they will help the sector you want to join.

5   Consider what do you need to start doing to make the overall experience more effective and to take you closer to achieving your goals. What strategies can you employ to make these happen?

Many people find work exhausting enough without doing career planning back home too. But this is where 110 per cent commitment and effort will get you to where you want to be, while the 90 per cent won't, so raise your standard.

How do you take time out to go for interviews?

Companies are paying for you to be there and do the job they need you to do, not to keep disappearing for interviews with others – who may be their competitors. If you keep calling in sick, this makes you look unreliable in the eyes of the agency *and* employer. Many companies will interview people first thing in the morning or late afternoon. Work extra hours the day before or after at your temporary assignment. Give your temporary employer as much notice as possible. Work at 110 per cent and they won't want to lose you. Ask your agency for advice as to how to best handle the situation.

Don't wait for doors to open for you. Get out there and start knocking on doors to connect to the opportunities you want.

If you want to set up a business while working, do it while others sleep

Consider the number of wannabe writers who rise at 4.30 a.m. to write in the hope they can chuck in the day job once they've hooked a book deal. If something is important enough to you, you'll *make* time for it, even if something else has to go. Keep the dream alive and work to turn it into reality.

Learn from others you deem to be successful – how do they do it?

Seek out those who are where you wish to be. They've done it. But *how did they get there?* People love to talk about themselves and many will see it as a compliment if you ask their advice. If they see passion and enthusiasm in you, they'll be more than happy to help.

Go to the major shows and exhibitions and talk to the exhibitors. How did they get to where they are today? What advice would they have for you? What has their career path been and what are the three most important factors which have contributed to their success? Contact designers and artists that you deem successful. What lessons have they learnt along the way that they can pass on to you? Follow up major show winners with an email to congratulate them and then ask their advice. Read Sarah Brown's book, *Moving on up*, with advice and stories from leaders in many sectors on how they got to the top and what it takes.

Get ahead – get a mentor

Mentors have been there, done it and got the t-shirt. They can be an invaluable source of help, advice and contacts and many mentors get a great deal from the process themselves. A mentor will talk to you about your goals, aspirations and how you can get there. They will help you stay on track and keep focused. There are lots of mentor programmes available through many specialist networking groups and you should look at various websites listed throughout this book to find one which suits your needs. Mentoring can be done face-to-face or over the telephone. If you want to get ahead, learn from those who will make you think about what you're doing, asking you questions which you wouldn't think of asking yourself.

Heading for self-employment?

Consider these questions:

* Name three companies which are success stories (they can be any size)?
* What makes them successful?
* What works well for them? What doesn't?
* What makes customers and clients turn to them for products and services?
* What can you learn from them and apply to your own business?

Now let's do this exercise differently:

* Name three companies which have not been successful or which are going through a really rough time?
* Where are they going wrong?
* What are they trying to do to put things right?
* What has put customers and clients off them for products and services?
* What can you learn from them and apply to your own business?

Brainstorm with friends or join forces with other graduates to see what you can learn from them and their outlook.

Have a go!

Opportunities to get a lucky break don't happen unless you work to create them. For example, BBC Talent run an annual competition for people trying to get into film and TV. If you don't enter, you're clearly not going to win. It's a competitive world out there. Get used to it!

Summary action points

Turn your experience from an academic one into a work-related one which means something to employers and gets you in the right mind-set.

1 Look to see how you can start living the working day so far as possible.

2 Identify steps you can take which will bring you closer to the role you want.

3 Review your progress to date in areas such as: your own self-awareness and how far that has come; your picture of your career and life in the next three to five years; how your network has changed; and how far you've researched potential employers (or courses) to apply to.

4 How can you change your behaviour to get the success you want? What could you do differently?

Chapter 7

Promoting yourself

The next stage, as you prepare to sell yourself, is to consider questions such as:

* What can you do to boost your chances of success?
* What can you control? What is outside your control? (For example, you can control the time you spend job hunting and where you choose to job hunt.)

If you respond to an advert in a newspaper, you *can* control the quality of your application, but you *cannot* control the numbers of applicants applying for the same post. You can choose to demonstrate your ability to communicate clearly and present your case well by submitting a well thought out, easily read and well expressed application.

Remember, enlist several ways of job hunting – don't put all your eggs into one basket. Aim to do something with each method at least once a week.

Once you've identified a vacancy, course or employer you want to go for:

1 Identify any deadlines so that you can work out what to do when, and pinpoint what needs to be done;
2 Assess the skills, knowledge, acumen and attitude your potential employer needs by researching their organisation carefully;
3 Identify the evidence you need to paint the picture of your capabilities and aspirations from your research, life resources,

characteristics to date, work experience, voluntary work, travel, leisure, team efforts and projects;

4   If you need to include a CV with your application, write it out until you are comfortable with it; produce a one page letter of application and anything else required. In your one page letter, highlight the skills and experience you have which are relevant to the role you are applying for, and explain why the company you are writing to appeals to you. Mention something about the company which shows you know a bit about them – perhaps a recent campaign they've designed for a client.

5   Before you send your application in, have it checked by someone else and copy it, so that you can refer to it before interview.

To save time, understand how companies recruit

If you are applying to a small company (50 people or less), the way to apply may be by sending a carefully thought through and well presented letter of application, together with a CD of your portfolio and your CV to the boss. Spell out what your qualifications mean to make life easy for them. Get rid of any educational jargon. Large companies will probably have a recruitment process that includes application forms, personality tests, telephone interviews, assessment centres, interviews and more, all organised by a graduate recruitment section.

If you have to complete an application form, and send a CV with it, it is tempting to put 'see CV' on many answers, which in itself could lead to your application being deleted. Application forms give recruiters an opportunity to compare applicants, so apply the 110% effort rule as opposed to 80 per cent. This rule also needs to be applied persistently and with rigour throughout the job hunting process. Remember that natural good manners can set you apart from other candidates throughout the process. No one wants to recruit someone who is rude, surly and sulky.

Submit an outstanding application, not just an excellent one

In the recruitment process, there is one winner, i.e. the person who is selected, who will stand out over the other applicants. The person who is selected will have probably given an outstanding performance from start to finish; the others may all be excellent, but in a competitive world, there is only one winner. So if you're going to put yourself a cut above all the other applicants, you need to make yourself stand out as an outstanding candidate.

Get physical

It's a competitive world out there, so prepare yourself to fight for your part in it. Exercise daily to sharpen your mind and body – the results will be apparent from your added energy and increased focus. Minimise the rubbish you eat and drink, including alcohol. Mental agility exercises will help you improve your ability to think on your feet.

Put yourself in the recruiter's shoes

Think about what you know about the company and the sector, and the role they are recruiting for. What are they looking for? What do they want? There are plenty of specialist books regarding CVs, application forms, applying online, assessment centres and the interview process and these are all listed under Further Information at the end of this book. Raise your standard over all the other candidates: invest a few hours in a good read. In addition, many agencies have hints and advice on their websites, so make the most of it.

Get practice in tests

If you know tests will form part of the assessment, ask your careers service for a practice run. Know what you're letting yourself in for; get used to handling questions, managing your time, and focusing on a task. The website www.prospects.ac.uk enables you to get your CV checked, talk to graduate employers and practice online personality and aptitude tests.

Five golden rules to kick off

1 Use a professional email address, putting your contact details at the bottom and use an appropriate header in the subject box, such as Graduate Opportunities. Address it to the right person; check their name on the company's website or by calling the switchboard.

2 Check your mobile and email regularly for messages. Recruitment can move quickly.

3 Make your application easy for recruiters to read; use bullet points, not prose. Explain your educational qualifications – spell out subjects you covered and the skills you've acquired.

4 On your CV, use a short opening statement of 30–40 words to describe your career aspirations, relating them to the role you're applying for or the company you'd like to work for. Describe the person who lies behind the CV or application form through your use of adjectives.

5 Paint the reader a picture of the scale of the projects or achievements you've worked on, using numbers, targets, deadlines, results, feedback and percentages. This will demonstrate your personal effectiveness in getting results. If your degree grants you exemptions to certain professional qualifications, say so. Be specific about the technology and computer applications you can use.

Business acumen, creativity and innovation are key aspects many employers will be looking for. They'll want customer focus, ideas, solutions to problems and challenges, and energy, drive, ambition and hunger to get things done and done correctly. Can you show that you've brought ideas to the table before and made them happen?

Make CVs personal and relevant to the company you're writing to

A CV should include headings for areas such as:
- Contact details (at the very top, easily spotted);
- Academic history (most recent first), pinpointing the most relevant aspects of your course to the employer and mentioning any exemptions from professional qualifications the course has given you, if relevant;

Table 7.1

Study	Extra-curricular activities
Work experience	Volunteering
Voluntary work	Travelling
Paid work	Projects
Leadership roles	Business activities at university/
Membership of societies	college

+ Work experience, which outlines projects you have worked on, and gives an idea of the size of each company you have worked for;
+ Overall achievements and positions of responsibility;
+ Interests and leisure – keep it brief and honest;
+ Personal details – for example, 'Willing to re-locate' if you are; a clean driving licence; marital status and age (use date of birth as opposed to age in years).

Pay particular attention to the way you lay out your CV, from the font size and type to the layout and way you organise the information you wish to portray. Keep it simple, but make it look good. Limit your CV to two sides or less. Send it by email or by post on paper (good quality white A4 with no gimmicks, designs, wrinkles or coffee stains). Don't put 'Curriculum Vitae' at the top – employers know what it is. Consider the sector you want to work in. Some, such as the professions – accountancy, banking, law, etc. – expect conventional CVs. Others, such as the media, expect candidates to be more creative with attention to layout and typescript, but not pretentious.

Many applications are wasted because they are riddled with spelling errors, hard to read and poorly researched. Others get a glance and perhaps go into a 'think about while reading the rest' pile. Some are easy to read and relevant, and then one or two will make the employer think *'There's that one line which makes me sit up and think, wow – I've just got to meet this person'*.

'They want one year's experience'

If you were to add up all your work experience and put it together on your CV, you may be surprised to find that it adds up to close to a year. Can you add to that paid and unpaid experience, commissions, contracts, work simulated projects, and voluntary efforts? Put all your work experience together in a CV and put it first before your educational qualifications so that it draws the employer's attention before anything else.

Outline your art or design experience

You should include details of exhibitions you've had (solo or otherwise), giving details of when, where and which gallery the event was held at. If you have had a number of these, choose the ones which you think are most relevant to the role you now want. Describe any commissions you have had, together with any awards you've won, work you've sold and articles or books you may have written. Give information which shows the scale of your achievements to a potential employer, giving names, dates, and details of the work involved. If you have a website, refer the employer to it. There you can include a brief description of each work, but not too much – you want them to be hungry enough to find out more about the person behind the ideas and pieces they see.

What happens after submitting your application?

As said before, for the small or medium-sized employer, you will probably need to send a CV and accompanying letter of application and then attend for an interview.

For larger firms, kick-off may involve sending in your CV or completing an online or paper application form, or perhaps doing an online psychometric test or personality questionnaire. Many employers then run initial screening by way of short telephone interviews with candidates. Regardless of who you're applying to, ask your housemates to answer the phone with greater courtesy than usual; explain that you're job hunting. Keep your details, a pen and paper by the phone, with a generic CV with your life history on it so you can quickly refer to grades you've obtained, if asked, or find information required.

Look at your potential: where do you want to be?

Where *do you see yourself in five years' time?* Who *do you want to become?* Increasingly, job prospects relate to the person you are and want to become (your potential), hence the heavy emphasis on psychological tests, assessment centres and even handwriting analysis in the recruitment process. It is not a good idea to say *'I'd like to be running my own company'* or *'I'll be travelling on a year off'* or *'I'd like to be in your job'*. Show ambition, but not at the expense of the interviewer, unless you're applying to a large company where there are clear ladders of progression. An employer will also want to know that you're a stayer. The recruitment process is a long and costly one, so they won't want to take on somebody who intends to leave within a year plus of joining, unless you move up their ranks.

This is a question that employers like to ask when recruiting and many job hunters think, *'Wow. I don't even know where I want to be next week! Why are these guys so hooked on this question?'* The thing to remember is that recruiting and training staff cost money and time and it's a risk. Employers need to know where your level of ambitions and drive are taking you, what your values and aspirations are and where you see yourself going. They need to look at the staff they are recruiting, to assess the spread of talents and skills they need and how you might fit and contribute to fulfilling their long-term vision, now and in the future. Large global organisations, for example, may have had to forecast their recruitment needs over a year ago. But many companies also recruit as the need arises, particularly if they are small, asking *'What could this person do for us starting from Monday?'* on the one hand, and wanting people who can grow with and contribute to the organisation on the other.

The fact that you have a degree shows your commitment to learning and developing yourself and realising your potential. An employer can see that by evidence of your conscious decision to study for a degree. They know you have the ability to learn and juggle life, study and work and progress. They can build on your strengths, weaknesses, skills, creativity, leadership abilities and management material. They can train you, probably promote you, give you a team of people to manage and expect results from you. They may provide financial and timely support for you to study towards professional examinations but they need to know that you can and will stand the pace of working relatively long hours during the weekday and studying at night. They'll look for the evidence in your application from start to finish.

More importantly, you and any potential employer need to know that you're right for each other. This is very much a two-way process. If you are not right for each other, it's far better to acknowledge it immediately. The way the organisation is structured may not enable you to meet your aspirations. Equally, if you're going on to further study, make sure you and the thing you are applying for, be it a course or role, is right for you and your long-term plans. Interestingly, this also applies if you want to set up your own business – know where you are and where you're going, and you're more likely to get there.

Post-graduate? Consider the difference ...

If you're a post-graduate, stand back and look at yourself from the time you completed your undergraduate degree and your post-graduate degree. Assess the difference the two made to you personally; what has changed about you and your approach as a result of your post-graduate studies? What particular skills, knowledge and breadth have you acquired from the second degree and how would that make a difference to an employer? What difference has it made to your character and personality, your strength, direction and self-belief? How can you sell those effectively to make a living from them or market them to employers? How can you show employers that you have extra fine-tuned skills in analytical thinking, communication, self-management and motivation and in the way you look at how things are done and how other people think, work and do things? Many students find that employers treat them the same as their undergraduate peers but, as the post-graduate, it is for you to take responsibility and make sure that your input and contribution is over and above what is expected of you.

Prepare to show your commercial awareness

Continue to research the sector you want to work in; industry news, who are the movers and shakers, who's who and which companies work in it. What sort of pressures are companies under? Where does the company fit into the sector and how does it stand out from its competitors? Why do they appeal to you over their competitors? Can you talk about its various products and services, their culture and ethos. How did they start and what has their growth been like? You want to join a company which is in the ascendent, not one which is spluttering and faltering, and starting to gasp for breath. Who are their main clients or customers and what have their recent campaigns, products and services been? What are the hot topics and issues of the day, and who is in the news and for what? Check share prices and read the last couple of annual reports to see how far the company is moving towards achieving its goals or vision. Pick up on the bigger picture by researching the company through the Internet and printed press, and talking to people who may know about it. Demonstrate you understand how organisations are organised and function. Your one-page covering letter of application can make a good start in showing this off as you outline why you chose to apply to the company over its competitors.

Show how you can benefit the company and fit in

Demonstrate that you have researched these points:

- What is the company's mission and vision?
- How does it expect to achieve that?
- What will it need to achieve it?
- What sort of drive and personal qualities from its employees will it need to be successful?
- What can you contribute to the organisation as works to achieve its vision?
- What does the consumer/client want?
- What are the trends and challenges facing the sector?
- What qualities will they be looking for in their employees? How can you demonstrate that you have them?
- What specific job skills does the recruiter call for that you can prove you have?
- What can you bring to the team that might be an added dimension?
- Are you ready to answer competency-based questions, with specific examples and to work through them in detail, giving employers a clear picture of how you approach problems and processes?
- Can you show that if they sponsor you for a professional qualification or a post-graduate course, that you'll commit to it in its entirety?

Each boss or line-manager has their own criteria to meet as they recruit for a role. These may refer to particular skills which are essential to the job, such as particular IT packages, and will assess every application throughout against these criteria; they may ask the same questions of all candidates to compare their answers. There may be someone from human resources there to check any legal requirements, to ensure that the other interviewers remain on track and ask appropriate questions, and to cover company benefits. Your prospective boss will look at your skills set and how they will fit with his requirements and, crucially, how you will fit in with the team. If you're applying for a small company, the boss and a member of the team may fulfil both roles.

Personal fit with the team

Well, you either fit, or you don't. And if you don't, it is more to do with the existing team as it is and the sort of person the selectors are looking to add to it. For this reason, you may be called back for several interviews with different members of the team to build up an all-round view of how you're going to fit in. View it each time as an opportunity to take a closer look at your potential colleagues. What would it be like arriving for work every day first thing in the morning and making small talk by the coffee machine? It is essential to be yourself throughout the process if this fit is to be right, real and genuine, so welcome each opportunity. Your colleagues will want to feel comfortable working with you on an assignment until three in the morning, and you'll want to feel good working alongside them.

Go into the recruitment process prepared to have fun

Most recruiters want to give you a good experience – they know you'll tell friends and family on what you thought of them. They know that if you are not in a situation where you can be yourself, they won't see the true you. The truth is that recruiters have a responsibility to take the right people on for the right roles, which is no easy task. Be prepared for the interviewer whose technique is appalling – rambling, non-stop, rude and arrogant. The website www.doctorjob.com can tell you more.

The assessment centre

Many (larger) companies use assessment centres to select their new recruits, lasting a morning or more to see how you'll cope with the demands and stresses of the job. They'll include activities such as team tasks and activities, numeracy and written tests, role-related tests (for example, creating an advert for a product if you were going into advertising), interviews and presentations, and company-specific tests. Look at each exercise from the employer's point of view. What competence or quality do you think they are looking for in the tests they have included? Focus on each one as it appears. Be prepared for the unexpected. You may be asked to present on a subject unknown to you, so that the selectors can see how you handle presenting, debating and working under pressure. Social events may not 'count' towards the assessment, but you'll be quietly watched to see how you interact. Find out what makes your potential work colleagues tick – will you want to be working with them every day under pressure? Drink an absolute minimum of alcohol. You want to be 110 per cent the next day while everyone else is at 80 per cent–90 per cent.

Attending an interview

If you decide to do freelance and contract work, you will need to sell yourself continually, so 'selling yourself' at meetings and interviews will become second nature to you. That said, some nerves are a good sign – they show you care. Preparing for an interview or assessment day takes place at several levels:

- Reviewing what you know about the sector you want to work in and the professional career you've chosen to follow (if relevant);
- Researching the company using every possible resource available to you. Visit any local stores or branches. Obtain brochures and read them carefully. What impression do they give you of the company? How comfortable would you feel having the staff there as colleagues?
- Reminding yourself of what you can contribute to that company and how it matches your career goals;
- Practical preparations, such as dressing the part, getting there with time to spare;
- Preparing mentally for questions you may be asked, such as What are your strengths? Tell us about a team effort you've contributed to and what your role was. Tell us about yourself!

- Preparing the night before – have an early night, keep alcohol to a minimum and don't eat anything with a strong flavour such as garlic.

Getting yourself in the right frame of mind. There's no point in taking baggage that spells the *'Oh poor me, I'll never get a job'* feeling. Leave it at home, put some music on which makes you feel really great en route, and focus on the task ahead. Remember, this interview is a two-way process and a chance for you to ensure that this employer is right for you, just as they need to make sure you're right for them.

A word about the *'Tell us about yourself'* question. This is not an invitation for you to recite your entire life history. Outline in a couple of sentences where you are now and where you want to be. Keep it short and throw them a couple of points they can pick up on.

Dress the part

Review your appearance. Is there anything you need to do, such as:

- Polishing shoes
- Getting shoes re-heeled
- Cleaning under your nails
- Getting a hair cut
- Making sure your suit isn't too tight or skirt too short
- Deciding what you could wear if you had to 'perform' two days running
- Looking for accessories which would enhance your image
- Not overdoing make-up, perfume or aftershave
- De-cluttering your handbag, so that you can find items easily in it
- Making sure your writing equipment – a pen and notebook – is easy to carry, professional, that your pen works and you have a standby.

Take along a copy of your CV, questions you have to ask, and any research you've found. Take directions of how to get there, and contact details of the person who organised the interview, in case you run into a problem en route. Charge your mobile phone. Account for potential problems on route when planning your journey times.

What sort of questions should you expect?

+ *Why us?*
  Be positive! Select two or three points which made them stand out against their competitors.
+ *What did you think of ...e.g. our brochure, website?*
  Be able to back up your views. Can you compare the product or service with those of the competitors in the sector?
+ *What do you think you'll be doing in the first year?*
  Comment on the research you've done through talking with other graduates and check your understanding of that role. Use the opportunity to ask questions you may have about that first year and your likely career progression.
+ *What is your perception of yourself?*
  This is all about how you think you present yourself to people. They may ask you how you think you present yourself to them. How do you want to appear?
+ *What achievement are you proudest of?*
  Think up several achievements before you go in and be prepared to talk about the work you put into making them so.
+ *What salary are you expecting?*
+ Outline the research you've done into salaries in the sector, both for new graduates and the industry as a whole. Be prepared to negotiate and remember that the added perks can affect the overall package considerably.

Remember, you're a graduate. On each point, show you've done your research and back up your answers with well thought out and cohesive answers which are clearly expressed.

Questions to ask the interviewers

Ask questions that will enable you to build up a picture of what sort of relationship you're likely to have with this employer and how your working day and week might look, both upon joining, six months after joining and then in about two to five years' time.

+ Is this a new position? If not, what is happening to the current post-holder? If the current post-holder is moving up or sideways, that's a signal of career progression; if the post is new, why has it been created? You need to ensure you're applying for a position which really is needed and has been thought through.

• Ask about the direction the company is taking – and how the company sees this post contributing to it.
• What training and career development will be available to you?
• Find out how long the interview process will take.

Whatever you do, be yourself

It is exhausting to keep up any pretence, and since both you and the company are trying to find out whether the two of you are suited to one another, it is also pointless. If you rapidly come to the conclusion that this company is not for you, then look at that as a positive. Have fun. Welcome the opportunity to test yourself, and be proud that you've got this far.

Offered the post!

Well done! Congratulations! Now, take a deep breath and consider the options ahead of you. Is this offer really what you want? Will you be happy walking into the organisation every Monday? Can you fulfil your short and longer-term career goals with it? Is the package right?

Add up perks and benefits

Perks vary, as employers provide increasingly individualised products and services for their employees, and much depends on size and sector, but Table 7.2 below shows examples.

Perks and benefits all add up. Find out how your salary is likely to increase in the future. Bonuses will vary according to the industry you're in and how well your company – and/or you – perform. Find out what the salaries are in the industry via recruitment agencies and salary surveys. Look at the kind of positions you would expect to hold in, say, three or five years' time and see what the salaries and perks are for them. How different are they to what you currently earn?

Table 7.2

Private healthcare	Joining bonus
Pension scheme	Personal accident insurance
Holidays	A sum of money to go towards a
Profit and performance related	course of the employee's choice
bonuses	Sharesave scheme
Buy or sell extra days holiday	Season ticket loan
Flexible working hours	Disability insurance
Child care discounts	Maternity and adoption phase-back
Discounted loans and mortgages	Summer shut down
Relocation packages	Company cars
Car lease schemes/discounts	Subsidised canteen
Financial support for professional	Language training
development	Sport and adventure training
Employee helpline	Insurance
Lifestyle managers	Travel cards
Pet insurance	Payment of professional association
Discretionary bonus	membership fees
Retirement plan	Work-wear
Social activities	

Going down the self-employed route

Consider where you're heading financially

What do you want to achieve financially through your art and design skills? Set yourself financial targets. Your bank or a business adviser can help you but you should have a clear idea of your costs, including equipment, your own pay, taxes and insurance, how much items will cost to produce, and what you'll charge for your products and services. And look at the examples of perks listed above, which are important to you long term and immediately? A bank loan may keep you watered, fed, sheltered and clothed.

How are you going to sell your work?

Like the writer, there's no point in your work languishing finished at the bottom of a cupboard, waiting for the day when 'it' will happen for you. Your work needs to be out there, selling itself and your talent, and as soon as it is finished, you need to start work on another and get that out in front of the public eye, too. You need to take a commercial viewpoint, as opposed to an artistic one, if you want to make a living from your talents and skills.

You need to find out which marketing and PR methods work for you and your business. There are many methods, such as:

* Forming a strategic alliance with shops, coffee houses, restaurants and galleries, health shops and gyms, who can show your work and perhaps even send out letters to their clients on your behalf explaining that your work will be showing;
* Attending art and craft fairs or country shows as a stand-holder, particularly if you have a niche. If, for example, you're an animal portrait painter, why not attend dog and cat shows?
* Giving talks to local groups about your work, a particular artistic element of your course, being a designer ... anything which will get people talking about you;
* Donating a piece of your work for a prize in a raffle;
* Donating your services as a prize in an appropriate raffle – for example, the opportunity to sell your designing skills in a business network lunch.

Think laterally and your potential market will expand. And always, always display your contact details.

Get out there and show your work off; make your name known

Whether you're an artist, craftsman/woman, designer, picture framer or offer an associated service, there are many sites which enable you to post pictures of your work on the web, where you can sell it commission free for an annual charge. You can display your work 24/7, advertise your exhibitions and have links to your own web address. You can include details about yourself, your background and work, plus examples from your portfolio, promote your exhibitions and anything else you offer. An online portfolio gives you the opportunity to reach buyers, agents, galleries and publishers worldwide. You can see if you can develop a strategic alliance with relevant companies on the Internet. You can also advertise directly to art societies, so that if you give demonstrations and talks, they can find you easily. You can include your fees and travel costs. Art clubs and societies are always looking for talented artists who can show their techniques in an interesting and entertaining manner. Why not make a CD Rom or video of what life is like at art college, and sell it on the Internet? Some sites charge, say, £5 per painting and they will have their own terms and conditions which you'll need to compare. Examples are www.artnetdirectory.co.uk and www.artyfarty.com. In the US, www.arts-crafts.com/ has listings of a wide variety of arts, crafts and designers with visitors from all over the world. It also has details of events taking place.

There are also specialist sites such as www.studiopottery.co.uk where you can provide details of yourself and images of your recent work, and details of galleries selling work and running exhibitions. It also has details of about 2000 events a year. It also has links to international organisations. The website www.ukpotters.co.uk is another example.

Write articles on the subject such as *'What it takes to enjoy your art'* or *'How to Get Creative'* or similar. Find out if you can take examples of your work along to local networking groups for display. Continually update your website with details of new work, exhibitions and news, plus new and relevant links. Keep track of who has bought your work and what appealed to them about it, how much they paid so that you have an idea of their price range, and email them information about new copies of your work. Email can easily be forwarded on, so even if your previous customer isn't interested, there's a chance he might forward it on to someone who could be. Can you develop off-shoots from the work which is selling well? Talk to people about what you're doing – see if you can get onto local radio, as stations often look for local people who are doing interesting things.

Running workshops and giving talks can be a great way to get your name known, but you need to find the right audience for your message. Find out what else is on offer in your area and work out what your unique selling points are and how you'll differ from your competitors. What can you offer that's added value? If you're temping and freelancing and working on your portfolio, you'll be amazed at how many people say, to you, *'I'd love to paint/draw/do something creative'*. Why not get them all together and run a workshop on a Saturday afternoon? People want to escape and do something different which is laid on for them, so why not create the opportunity for them and charge a small fee to cover your costs and outgoings? (Find out if you need to take out insurance for the event.)

Summary action points

Once you've started sending applications or taking steps towards your proposed first career move after your degree:

1 Keep a record of what you're sending out and when; this will help you to ascertain whether you're doing enough towards your goal;
2 Assess what is working particularly well and build on that;
3 Obtain feedback where you can to help you to improve your performance the next time;
4 Get involved in a couple of things in life other than careers and job hunting to help keep a balance in your day and week.

Chapter 8

What's stopping you?
Make it happen!

Frequently in life, things seem to take far too long to go our way. We're waiting for that great job, or know that there isn't going to be one in the region we are in. We're waiting for a lucky break. But all too often, we are the people who stop ourselves getting what we want in life.

There are varying scenarios that befall us. For example, you can fall into a rut. You feel that you need a boost with the firepower of a space shuttle to get out of it, followed by a long sustained blast of persistent rocket fuel-type effort. This doesn't just happen in your career, but in relationships with people; perhaps the excitement has gone out of a relationship and you need a super-boost of impetus and excitement to bring it back to life. Perhaps your ability to be spontaneous in life has been overtaken by a preference for the known, safe and comfortable.

It may be that the situation you're in needs one bold, decisive step to get to where you want to be, but you feel like taking that step is like being asked to ski down the steepest, highest most icy slope. You just need to push yourself over the edge and set off, but it's making that first push which freezes you. At this point, we often fear failure and of looking like a fool in front of others – but we also fear success. We procrastinate from making that call, for fear of being turned down, rejected – but what if we succeed? How will we handle the changes in life that will invariably follow? Will we cope with them?

And then we make glorious plans, and life gets in the way. Family problems, a friend in trouble, illness, death, redundancy, changes thrust upon us, rows ... they all combine to be the reasons why we are where we are.

And sometimes, it seems that we aren't getting anywhere or at least where we want to be as quickly as we wish. Maybe we're waiting for that magic breakthrough – selected at interview, obtaining funding for that post-graduate course, securing an introduction and follow-up meeting with an employer you really want to work for, having a business idea while in the shower. We're waiting, confident that these things will happen one day. If we don't stay on top of things and create the right environment and conditions for success, we will probably wait a long time.

Don't forget what you went to university for!

If your career plans are taking an age to come to fruition, it can be really frustrating to see all those successful people at work who didn't go to university who say, 'Well, university wasn't for me, and now I'm a millionaire several times over'. It can be easy to fall into the trap of blaming others for your current situation, thinking and saying things like 'Well, the school pushed us into it', and 'My parents thought it would be a good idea'.

Five survival tips are:

1 Recognise that there are gifted people who chose not go to university but who have made it up the ladder by another route – people reach their potential in their own way and time; what matters is that they get there.
2 Keep everything in perspective – you have as much chance of succeeding as they do.
3 Learn from them.
4 Recall what you got out of your university days. No one can ever take them away from you, or your degree.
5 Focus on where you want to be. Review the progress you've made so far and assess how far you've moved towards achieving your main goals. Identify what else you need to do.

Dig deeper into your resources

Whether you fall into a rut or you need to take that one decisive, courageous step, there will always be stages in your life where you need to get tough with yourself and dig deeper within you for the resources you need to achieve the result you want. These resources usually come from within us: energy, focus, clarity of vision and action required, determination, an ability to go out there and get on with it. You've done it before, when you chose to apply to university – and then when you packed up and left home to head out there. It is the time to look afresh at the way you spend your time and energy and to get any unwanted stuff out of the way, such as anything that pulls you down.

Strengthen your resolve

You can choose to change your attitude, approach and luck, and you'll have subconsciously done so many times in your life when you felt good about what you were doing, things were going well, and you were on course for where you were heading. You may not have been aware that you were doing them. Since then, you probably picked up some bad habits, so it's a good time to make sure they aren't holding you back.

Dump the 'I'll try'. Trying isn't the answer

You can train yourself to think positively and talk positively by watching your language. If you're planning to do something, and think 'I'll try to do this before lunch tomorrow', then in fact you're unlikely to do it. Think 'I will do this tomorrow before lunch', and you inject a whole new energy into your focus and you're far more likely to get the thing done. Watch your language for a morning and listen for positive and negative statements. If you're talking more negatively than positively, that will be affecting your mood and manner. You can change that by simply talking more positively and changing your state and the way you're feeling.

What message are you taking on board?

Sometimes we don't help ourselves. If we're feeling down, and we watch a depressing television programme in which people are rowing and living mediocre lives, that's going to make us feel worse. If we listen to a piece of music we love and which makes us feel great and fantastic, then our approach to life changes. Aim for the positive and get a lift from it. Assess the information you receive in any format, dump the negative, work with the positive and strive for the possible and realistic.

Are you caught up in unhelpful patterns of thinking and behaviour?

Examples include criticising yourself, imposing limits or boundaries on the opportunities before you. It involves giving yourself excuses for failing before you start, spending more time on socialising than job hunting, so not giving your career the prominence in your life that it deserves. Perhaps you're being too influenced by listening to generalisations from people who don't know what they're talking about; or you're not applying any creativity to your problem to find a solution. Either way, you make the choice whether to take those on board and listen to them, or not.

Misunderstanding by others of what graduates can do for them

This is particularly the case in the SME market, where many bosses cannot keep up-to-date with all the changes in education at any level, unless they are parents. So make it easy for them. Pay particular attention to your work experience when you write your CV and paint as clear a picture as you can for them of what you can do with clear examples.

Use your problem-solving skills

What can you do to solve the problem?

1 Identify a problem or issue you have now, such as finding that first right role, making your business work, or paying off your student debts.
2 Revise where you are now with the problem and identify the solution you want.
3 What is happening right now?
   - What are you doing which is working for you?
   - You've tried everything? Okay, ask yourself:
     - What exactly have you tried?
     - How often have you tried it?
     - When specifically?
     - How much time did you spend on it? How carefully did you do it?
     - What is working well? What isn't?

* Look back over the last seven days. What did you do on each of those seven days to tackle the problem? If you only spent an hour on Monday and Wednesday doing something, you cannot expect to solve it.

  If you learn from this exercise that you're only spending two hours a week making new friends, but that friendship is important to you, then something in your week needs to change. You may need to sacrifice something else to allow room for the change to happen. If you want to work on your portfolio but only devote three hours a week to it, and four evenings to going out with friends, although your social life is going to look pretty good, your portfolio won't. Devote four evenings to your portfolio, and that fifth evening spent with friends really will feel well deserved.

4   What extra resources and skills do you need to make the change happen? Table 8.1 below gives hints! Where will you get them from?

5   Look for new solutions.

* Brainstorm every single thing you can think of that you might do to change the situation to make it just the way you want it to be.
* What one thing do you need to do differently to get the results you need?
* What else could you do?
* What other ways could you approach the issue?
* What would you advise a friend to do?
* Who do you know who is where you want to be now?
* What help and advice could they offer you?
* Who might have experienced the same problem before and could help you unblock where you are now by acting as a mentor to you?
* If you're running your own company, what could you do to market yourself?

Table 8.1

Extra	Contacts
Skills	Knowledge
Time	Experience
Energy	Influence
Qualifications	Materials
Opportunities	

6   Finally, identify the actions you are prepared to take and when yo Holidays u're going to take them. Pinpoint any support you'll need and identify where you can get that from.

Focus on what you can change

Do something about the things you can change and don't waste time worrying about the things you cannot. When you look at the graduate recruitment market and your life after graduation, identify the things you can influence. If you're self employed, look at the way you organise your resources because you can influence the way you access and use them.

Pinpoint the missing angle which, once added, could lead to success

What do you need to do to turn your current position into a success and get to where you want to be? For example, you could consider:

1   Working for employers who naturally take on students with one or two years' experience after university. Why not find out how this route into the workplace would help you? Here your alumni associations with your old university could be invaluable.

2   Moving into an allied profession for a couple of years and then a change of track later, either in your own country or abroad.

3   Relocating now to where the opportunities are – which could be further afield than you like.

4   Working part time or on short-term stints until you find the right position. Go freelance!

5   Discussing your situation with relevant professional organisations; how flexible are the rules and regulations governing entry to and qualification for membership?

6   Starting your own business. There are lots of opportunities and programmes around for graduates who have business ideas, so find out what support and finance might be on offer and brainstorm that business idea!

7   Joining forces with fellow students from your course and brainstorm the issue together. What could you do collectively to turn the current situation into an opportunity?

Boost your creativity into solving problems and looking for opportunities. Get friends to help you brainstorm, and tap into their knowledge and creativity too.

What practical steps can you take?

There could be practical steps you need to take to blow barriers away. Let's look at some of them.

Identify your skills gaps

Look at anything which may boost your employability. For example, you could show your CV to a designer and ask whether there is anything they think that's missing from your CV to get you into the work you need. A CAD course might be just the ticket, if you haven't done one already. You can study for CAD part time or full time at a local college near you. You can also follow self-paced CAD courses with www.autocadcourses.co.uk. Some CAD courses are sector specific, such as the CAD Course for Landscape Designers, run by Oxford College of Garden Design (www.garden-design-courses.co.uk).

In many cases, it won't be your skills which are at a loss. It will be your experience or own organisational skills which are missing. Pinpoint where the gap is between where you are and where you want to be and work out what you need to do to fill it. That gap could consist of particular skills or knowledge.

While waiting for a response ...

One of the traps writers tend to fall into is that they will send out a proposal to a publisher or editor and then wait for a response. What they should be doing is congratulating themselves for getting a proposal out, and then heading straight back to their desks to work on the next one. Don't fall into the same trap. As soon as you've finished work on one application, start on the next.

Keep working at your craft, whatever it is. There will be days when you wonder how on earth you can keep going and when you'll get your lucky break, especially if you're combining your art and design work with another job to keep the money coming in. Stand back and taking a long-term approach but ensure that you work continually towards your end goal. Continually add to your experience, ideas, portfolio and CV. Keep coming up with new creations, designs and ideas. Get your skills and talents out on show; don't tuck them away where no one can see them. Offer to do something for a local charity or business for free – you can talk about it at interview and you can show that you understand the importance of talking to the client and taking their views on board, that you have kept the bottom-line in mind and worked with a team to see an idea through the conception stage and on to completion.

What specialist help is about to help you overcome any barriers you're hitting?

Many groups with special needs now have their own support networks, such as those who have had cancer or heart problems, mature workers, ex-offenders, those returning to the work after a break, people with disabilities, those with learning difficulties, asylum seekers, ethnic minorities, women – the list is simply endless. There are sites set up to help you, such as www.ndaf.org, the National Disability Arts Forum, which has links to many local groups and enables people with a disability to sell their work online.

How well are you promoting yourself?

Think about the way you're selling yourself in terms of your approach, enthusiasm and passion for the industry. You need to show yourself as a person who can be trusted in the way you handle people and situations. Construct whole sentences, rather than using texting language that you'd send to your friends and family. Do not call people 'mate', 'darling' or any other form of endearment. They are not your 'mates'.

Some simple do's and don'ts now follow. Patronising? No, they are merely included because of employers' comments regarding the lack of basic social skills and manners in many graduates. Practice a warm firm handshake with your friends, looking people in the eye. Keep your shoulders back and square and your head up. You can practice this with strangers you meet in everyday life. When you meet new people, use this handshake and smile. Drop the grunt;

you're a graduate: sell yourself as such. Show yourself to be a positive, can do person. Leave the moods at home. We all get black days but there is no need to bring them to work. Do not whine about your current situation or blame past employers, teachers or anyone else for the state you are in. Be positive about going to university. You chose to do it and you gained from it, even though it may not seem like it right now.

Common Concerns

I've just got a 2:2 …
You're lucky. I've only got a third …

Well, many employers are stipulating that yes, they do want a 2:1 or above and some are quite adamant that they won't consider anyone with lower than that. But there are plenty of good employers out there who will and your task now is to focus not on what you cannot change but what you can do and influence to get your foot in the door. Focus on what you can offer in the way of key skills, personal qualities and drive and motivation – things you can promote and sell to an employer who will want to know how you can contribute in the future. Could you work for that employer in a couple of years' time after getting some relevant experience behind you?

What about my age?

If you omit your age from your CV or application, employers will wonder even more about your age. Use your date of birth (not your age e.g. 44 years) – it takes longer to work out so people are less likely to bother until later – and put it towards the end of your CV so that the recruiter can be excited about what you have to offer first. But, there are plenty of good things about being a mature worker and you should show that you mix easily with younger people (not mentioning children or grandchildren) in working situations, that you believe you can learn from each other, and get your image checked to make sure you look smart, crisp and fresh. Emphasise your work experience and the good points about maturity; many employers find mature staff more reliable. Show, too, that you can handle change well and that you're not stuck in your ways.

Being successful abroad

The key to success with a move abroad is to immerse yourself totally into the culture and to meet as many locals as you can. If you stick with people of your own nationality, you might as well have stayed at home. Learn a little of the language before you go, at least enough to be able to say some pleasantries; if you can, talk to people who've worked there so that you know what to expect and what the differences will be. Take pictures of your family and friends to show new friends that you're human too. Enrol in a language school when you arrive to boost your skills. Read the local papers to find out what's happening and observe local customs and, in particular, dress. Ultimately, you want to win people over rather than alienate them. Watch, listen and observe and see what you can learn from people.

Learn from failure

If you're going to succeed in work, either as an entrepreneur or an employee, you need to be tough and tenacious, and to learn from failure. Two-thirds of all start ups fail in the first three years, for example, but many successful entrepreneurs point out that failure can be a tremendous learning tool. Failures give up their dreams and goals. They don't learn from the experience because they don't even try to see where they went wrong. They usually fall into the blame culture. Winners and successes may fail, but they learn from their failures and take the experience forward to build future successes.

Analyse failure, and you move forward. View it as part of the learning curve of life, and you'll come out much stronger for it. The tough times in life show you that you have what it takes to survive and come out of situations on top. As you get older, you realise how much you've grown from all those difficult times in work and personal lives. We all hit rough patches in life, like an aircraft going through turbulence, but we usually come out of it all the stronger for it. When you look back on something in this context, if you learn from an experience, you can hardly describe it as failure.

Don't take failure personally

If you didn't get that much cherished job you wanted, perhaps it simply wasn't meant to be – maybe someone else was simply a better fit for the post and the company. Take your 'failure' with you in the

next interview and you won't win any friends. Invest in a punch bag or have a workout in the gym instead, obtain feedback if you can and review your performance yourself.
Ten survival steps to coping with failure

1   Have faith in yourself – there will be that perfect position for you somewhere out there, but you need to know what you're looking for. Keep focused and keep trying.
2   Keep knocking at doors. Get help and support around you, both experts in the field and your friends and family.
3   Ask for advice on turning those potential applications into sure bets.
4   Look for new strategies.
5   Keep a sense of perspective.
6   Don't turn to comfort eating, drink or drugs. It won't make change anything. Keep healthy.
7   Learn from those who have failed but picked themselves up and gone on to be successful.
8   Obstacles in our way are often our unwillingness to say 'no' to people, or our belief in ourselves as much as anything real or physical.
9   Push yourself out of your boundary zone at every opportunity you get. You'll be surprised how much you can achieve.
10 Live life differently if you can. A fresh approach works wonders and avoids your getting stuck in a rut.

Self-employed and ...

Someone's pinched my idea!

If you're going to create and implement designs or ideas or anything of that ilk, you'll want copyrights, patents and trademarks. Protect your own ideas and designs by making full use of the support available to you, such as:

ACID – Anti Copying in Design: www.acid.uk.com
Institute of Trade Mark Attorneys: www.itma.org.uk
Usability Professionals' Association: www.upassoc.org
Own It: www.own-it.org

Finally, the Charter on Intellectual Property promoted a new user-friendly way of handing out intellectual property rights in 2005, written by an international group of artists, scientists, lawyers, politicians, academics and business experts.

Access to finance

Apart from the obvious organisations to try, such as professional bodies and trade organisations, don't forget to tap into the various initiatives which may be taking part in your country or region to encourage growth and regeneration. The Arts Council has details of grants available for the arts (at www.culture.gov.uk/arts/funding_for_arts/default.htm) or you could tap into regional sources of funding such as www.advantagecreativefund.co.uk if you live in the West Midlands. You could also visit www.artquest.org.uk which has a lot of very useful information on many subjects as well as funding.

Needing help on a particular aspect of your journey?

Certainly in the UK, the creative industries sector is enjoying huge growth in many parts of the country. A consequence of that is that many cluster groups develop, by which artists and designers in the broadest sense of the word can meet with colleagues and other like-minded professionals, share best practice and benefit from each other's experience, expertise and network. Many of these will have individuals you can tap into for expert help and advice. These vary in the way in which they are organised and in the help they can give you. BusinessLink's network can help you, firstly, to set up your own business, and secondly, to grow the business, with help and information in areas such as exploiting your ideas, employing people, health and safety, premises, international trade, finance, grants and guidance on the rules and regulations applying to businesses in the creative industries sector.

Not getting the commissions?

Think about what is working for you and what is not. Contact people who have decided not to buy or pursue your product or service, and ask for some feedback. Is there anything in your sales pitch which did not endear them to your sale? What could you have done differently to achieve a different outcome? If there was nothing, were you looking in the right place for clients to start with, or pricing it properly? Obtain business advice, either from local business advisers or specific industry bodies.

Summary action points

Identify barriers and obstacles and then do something about them through creative thinking.

1 Identify what barriers and obstacles you have ahead of you which may hinder you achieving your goals.
2 Now pinpoint as many ways to tackle them as you can.
3 Identify the one which will work best for you and do it.

Chapter 9

Moving on ... Your future

No matter who you work for, careers and businesses need nurturing and loving care just like any relationship in life. If you look after them, devote time and energy to them and focus on them, they will blossom. You need to give your career loving care, or it will degenerate into just a job.

First, though, you need to walk before you can run

So you've signed up, started work, and you know you're expected to hit the ground running and adjust to the workplace culture as quickly as you can. What can you do to make this easier for yourself?

Ask if you can go into the office and spend a couple of hours meeting colleagues before your official start date. This will give you a chance to find where things are (e.g. coffee machine, etc.) and get familiar with the area, so that you know where to get a sandwich for lunch, the nearest chemist, newsagent, etc. It will make the place seem less unfamiliar when you have that first day. Check the dress code (which you may or may not have had a chance to observe during the assessment process). If you're at all unsure, watch people leave the building and see how they are all dressed. Check your working hours, starting time for the first day, and whom you should report to. Work out what you're going to wear each day in that first week and make sure it's clean, pressed and that there are no buttons hanging off. Organise your meals for the week, so that you don't have to think about what to eat at night or buy food on the way home.

However nervous you are, be yourself and keep smiling. Most people recall what it was like on their first day; they will want to put you at ease. Remember that you need to put in a sustained effort, so don't burn yourself out by being over-enthusiastic and friendly in the first few hours. If you're working for a large company, ask for a buddy who can help and guide you if you have questions about the place, someone you can turn to for advice and information. Talk to people at the coffee machine and join them for lunch if you can. They are human, after all, and you're hoping for a relatively long association with them as friends and colleagues.

As you meet people, a friendly firm handshake will do. Don't make this too firm and hearty, or give anyone a hug. Find out about the company policy regarding mobiles and personal emails; and before you put any information online, such as blogs, consider how it could be used. Keep your own counsel; don't shoot your mouth off. Pick your confidantes and true work friends with care. Confidential means just that.

Starting work in any company can be frustrating for a few weeks. You want to prove yourself and settle in. Yet being in a new work environment is just like being in a country you've never visited before, with lots to learn: how the computer system works, and whether there is an intranet; whose approval you need for what; who the key decision makers are; what the arrangements are vis-à-vis coffee and tea breaks/where you get them/whether you pay for them; and what people do at lunch time. You'll also learn who is who, what is where, and try to remember names and what people do.

Make an impact!

Eight ways to do this are:

1   Be friendly without being gushingly so. Don't call people 'mate'. They are not your mates (yet); they are work colleagues;
2   Listen and learn how things work before you dive in with comments; it can help to find out the history behind something which looks strange to you before you make suggestions;
3   Ask people questions about themselves and their role. *What do you do? How long have you been here?*' It's a great way to make friends at work and learn who does what;
4   Be willing to stay late to get things done;
5   Double-check your work for accuracy;

6   Prove you're a safe pair of hands to be trusted and a team player who fits in. Take your turn getting the coffee, if that's what people do;

7   Be ready to begin at the bottom and use the opportunity to learn as much as you can about the way the organisation functions;

8   Get social. Hang about and talk to people, have a coffee or drink with them.

As well as working, there's the added stress of handling full-time work five days a week, and doing all those small but essential tasks needed to keep life ticking along smoothly. If you spend eight hours a day sleeping (56 hours a week) and nine hours a day working, including the commute to work, that leaves you with 67 hours a week to do your admin, paying bills and banking; laundry and ironing, cleaning and shopping, cooking, eating and washing up, personal hygiene and, more occasionally, check ups with the doctor, dentist, hygienist and gynaecologist, and taking the car to the garage for an MOT. You'll also want time to enjoy activities such as socialising, catching up with old mates, remembering your parents, leisure hobbies, exercise, having weekends away and that all important 'me' down time to relax and re-charge your batteries. On top of all that, you may have enrolled for further learning or work towards a professional qualification.

Studying for professional qualifications or a part-time post-graduate degree?

If you've decided to study for professional qualifications, talk to your current employer to find out what support they can give you. This may take a number of forms such as study leave or financial support, perhaps paying for all or part of the course, or your study materials or examinations. When approaching the subject, look to show how far the studies will boost your effectiveness on the job and benefit your employer, so that you present a 'win–win' situation.

Professional bodies should have information online regarding continued professional development, including which institutions are accredited to offer which course. Some have mentors who can help you with your time management and learning organisation, both essential ingredients to success.

Work out the time which is best for you to study. The time could be late at night, in the early hours of the morning or at the start of a new day. You know when you work best and at your most effective. It requires real motivation and dedication to do this. There will be many occasions when you just feel like switching off and doing something totally different or even nothing at all. Get advice from those who've been there before to learn from those who've done it. Find a quiet place and time to study and reward yourself afterwards. Above all, keep the reason you're studying for the qualifications at the forefront of your mind, because it will keep you going when times get tough.

It's not working out!

If you think things aren't going well as you try to settle into a new job, give it time. Ask for feedback on your performance and try to identify what it is that is not quite right. Perhaps time will help you settle or it could be that you need more support from your boss or line-manager. If that is not the case, view this role as a stepping stone to something better. It can take a couple of attempts to get the match of employer and role right; many employers appreciate that. In fact, some even deliberately take on graduates a couple of years after their degree, with the understanding that their first post may not have lived up to their expectations or worked out.

So what happens next?

There are a number of 'what' and 'where' and 'how' questions here. What have you achieved so far, and where do you see your career going next? Are there any potential barriers or obstacles which might hinder your progress? Can you acquire extra skills to give you more openings in the employment market? If you are working for an industry which thrives on employing freelancers, you will need to be particularly proactive in networking and promotion yourself. Some websites, such as Skillset, have advice for people who have been made redundant or pages to offer support to freelancers. Much of it is relevant to the creative industries overall. It has lots of useful information on your rights, as well as financial matters, and it talks you through the various stages with great clarity and support.

A dogged, persistent effort is essential to take you to career success, in which these skills will be essential:

- *Self-awareness*
  Knowing your strengths, weaknesses, passions, ambitions, values and needs
- *Self-promotion*
  Raising your profile in the organisation and sector
- *Exploring and creating opportunities*
  Being pro-active in taking responsibility for your own career development
- *Decision making and action planning*
  Making informed, decisive decisions that will take you in the right direction, and working out what needs to be done and when
- *Coping with uncertainty*
  Dealing with redundancy, restructuring, new clients, new tomorrows
- *Transfer of skills*
  Thinking laterally and broadly, applying the commonalities to the workplace and life
- *Self-belief and confidence*
  Yes, you can do it!
- *Willingness to learn*
  New products, new technology, new skills
- *Commitment/dependability*
  Everyone knowing you're a safe pair of hands, and management and your own staff trusting you
- *Self-motivation*
  Having drive and enthusiasm, and taking the initiative
- *Co-operation*
  People wanting to have you on board their team
- *Communication skills*
  Making yourself clearly understood in the right way and through various means
- *Knowledgeable about new developments in the field*
  Showing that you're up-to-date

Plot and plan your next steps effectively, pinpointing the learning and experiences you will need to get to the next stage, especially if you are in a lower level position than you had hoped for after leaving university. Set a long-term goal and break it down into manageable steps. Keep these at the forefront of your mind. While everyone else sleeps and parties, work at your goal. You'll soon climb the career ladder through your own dogged determination, persistence and perseverance while they are left dozing or snoring their way through the working week. Failures in life give up. Winners persist.

Getting promoted

If you want to move up, plan for it so that you can prepare a path. For instance, if you get the chance to train any new staff or take responsibility for a group, do it; such an action will give your employer a chance to see how you put your management skills into action. Ensure your team knows what is expected of them and treat them all fairly and equally. When you delegate, check that people know what needs to be done, by when, and ask if they need any help. Explain why the task is important. Listen to their feedback and questions. Show how effective you are and tell your boss about the results you're getting. Watch the behaviours of those higher up and ask them what has worked for them.

Smooth the path to promotion

Make sure you have a regular review, so that you can work out how to improve your performance, assess how you're progressing and where your career is heading within that organisation. You can check that you're on track to achieve your career goals in the time-scale you want. Continually review the way you work – how can you handle your work-load more effectively and time efficiently while maintaining or improving your performance? Ensure you understand what your new role is about and what it contributes to the organisation's vision. Check that your team understands their mutual role, too. Are they properly trained and motivated to achieve the results expected of them? As you progress up the ladder, put a managerial hat on, rather than the technical, and take a higher helicopter view looking at the bigger picture. Delegate where you can, developing those you supervise through coaching, mentoring and one-to-one training. Assess whether you need any extra skills or qualifications to progress your path, such as an MBA or a postgraduate or professional studies. And consider how changes at work could provide you with new opportunities.

A strong network right across a company could smooth your path into new roles and it will raise your profile. Get on a committee so that other people can see how you perform. Keep up-to-date with everything that is going on in your sector and in your clients' sector. Be the first to know. Finally, dress for the role you aspire to, not the role you're in.

Are you working for a small company?

Sit down with the boss every six months or so to review your progress and the results you have achieved. Then talk about your career progression. Look to build up your skills and experience – can you take on more, for extra reward? Is there a project you can get into which will give you the experience you need?

And outside the office ...

Networking is as important outside a company as you climb the career ladder as it is in it. Many senior managers and professionals are recruited through recruitment agencies, head-hunters and search companies. These companies receive assignments from organisations which have roles to fill. Headhunters will call around their contacts in the industry to see if they know of anyone who might fit the bill. Someone in your network may think of you ...

Know your worth

Prior to your reviews, find out what the industry pays someone with your experience and qualifications, but don't forget that perks can make a huge difference to the overall package. Many agencies have salary reviews on their websites, so check out companies specialising in your sector for up-to-date pay trends. Pull all your evidence together of what you've contributed to the company, plus your research on salary and put your case forward for a rise if you want one. Don't expect to get an immediate answer and don't be surprised if the answer is no, but be prepared to negotiate. Perhaps the company will pay for you to undertake further studies instead of having a salary increase. There are ways and means to enhance your overall package.

Make the most of your professional body

Many professional bodies have different types of membership depending on the stage you are at in your career. Are you progressing your level of membership to match your experience? Can you get involved in a working group to boost your network and knowledge and influence the direction it takes, or get involved in your region and give something back to those young professionals coming through?

Continue to train and learn

You'll need to learn both in and outside work throughout your life. A report called *Who Learns at Work?* produced by the Chartered Institute for Personnel and Development in the UK in 2005 shows that people do not take up training because they don't have enough time, or their family and personal commitments prevent them from doing so; others lack the motivation to do it, or their manager prevents it. View training as an investment, or an insurance if you like, which boosts your employability.

As a graduate, you're more likely to ask for training because you are used to identifying your own training and learning needs and making sure they are met. Your university studies will have taught you how to learn through many methods, which will prepare you well for training at work. You can learn informally, by reading books and articles, taking correspondence courses, accessing learning materials on the Internet and also more formally for a qualification. You can also learn by being shown how to do things and then practising them, or through one-to-one training and coaching sessions with a manager or boss. Identify where your skills gaps are and what you need to do to close that gap. Think about skills which will give your company or your own performance an added dimension and get you ahead of the rest.

In the UK, the newly formed Design Council Advisory Panel recently worked to produce a workforce development plan to ensure employers have the skills they need. Visit www.design-council.org.uk for more information. Their report was due in the spring of 2006, and will help ensure UK industry remains competitive in the global economy.

Continued Professional Development (CPD)

The new Sector Skills Council for the creative industries is working to ensure employers have the skills they need in the future, and that education and training systems match the requirements employers have. For example, visit the website www.creativepeople.org.uk; Creative People is a network of organisations which provides advice and guidance to support the professional development of those working in arts and crafts industries. It offers advice, information and guidance to current and wannabe art and craft practitioners. Skillset offers freelance training for freelancers. Visit Visiting Arts (www.visitingarts.org.uk/training/index.html) which organises training, placement and residency programmes for artists, art managers and practitioners coming to the UK. There are plenty of programmes for artists and designers, such as www.ft2.org.uk/ offering film and television freelance training. If, for example, you have been in this particular industry for a number of years, you can have your skills and experience assessed and thus acquire recognition and qualifications through the Experienced Practitioner Route or EPR. You do this through your CV and witness statements given by professionals in the industry with the appropriate experience and status.

In the UK, Creative Learning Accounts may put purchasing power into the hands of the sole creator or freelancer – you can buy from preferred network of preferred courses and suppliers. Ultimately, this will contribute towards a Skills Passport.

Essential CPD

It may be essential for you to continue with your learning and training after you've achieved professional status on an annual basis. This helps keep you up-to-date with new technologies, skills, developments and knowledge and you should discuss your needs with your employer or contact the most relevant professional body to assess what you need to do to meet this commitment. Invest time in training and continued development – it's a great way to put fresh impetus into your work and career and will help ensure continued career progression. Plan your CPD well ahead in the year to ensure that you meet any necessary targets and can truly select something which will enhance your learning.

Consider learning a language

Employers are increasingly aware of the benefits of having a workforce who can talk to customers and clients in their own language. In this small world, there is an increasing belief that senior executives need to be bilingual or multilingual to succeed in today's business world. It will become more important for executives to be at least bilingual and a significant competitive advantage for executives to be multilingual. If you can speak your customers' language, they will appreciate it, and working life is all about putting the customer's needs first.

Leaving your current employer

If you think you're coming to a dead-end in your current role, take stock of where you are. Before you hand in your notice, ensure that there are absolutely no other opportunities at your current company. Consider what you have done to create opportunities for expanding your role and taking on new projects and responsibilities. What is right with the job you have now? Often there's plenty we like about our work, and it's the bits we don't like that we tend to focus on and gripe about.

Now look forward. Have your ambitions got lost in the current role you're in? Before you decide whether you can achieve them with your current employer, talk to your boss and/or human resources and put an action plan together to help you get back on track. If your current employer cannot meet your future aspirations, then research a move to another organisation or setting up business on your own. Get the new deal signed before giving in your notice. Be discreet, and don't work at your CV in work time on a work PC. Use the Internet and specialist agencies, your network and company websites to help you find that next right move.

Relocating abroad

If we choose to work abroad, many of us would like to think that we can go back to our homes after years away. Keep an eye on developments in your home country to make sure that time spent away doesn't prevent you from returning to your home country of birth, buying a house, settling down or anything else. When you're looking at any financial provision for your future, check to see what the taxation implications are if you move about. How will working abroad affect any pension due to you later in life, for example, be it state or private? A good accountant with international experience should be able to help you. Shop around to get the best deal you can.

So you've set up your own business and want to go for growth?

As you grow, delegate as much as you can, so that you're free to focus on the business. One possibility is to hire a virtual assistant, whom you would pay by the hour. Visit the website www.iava.org. uk to find out more.

Consider these questions:

* What have you achieved to date?
* What are your strengths, weaknesses, opportunities and threats?
* Where do you see your business going in the next year? The next five years?
* What extra resources do you need, e.g. time, money, equipment?
* Who can help you with that?
* What new products or services are you creating/innovating?
* What extra staff if any do you need and how will you find and employ them?
* What are you doing to build your niche and brand?
* What are your financial targets for the year?
* How much time are you devoting to business planning?
* What can you outsource, leaving yourself to focus on developing the business?
* What are you doing to get feedback from your customers to enhance the prospect of repeat business?
* Which marketing methods are proving to be most effective?
* What three new ways can you think of to market your business?
* What three new things can you think of to surprise and delight existing customers?
* Which comes first: business or lifestyle?

Look at the examples of perks listed earlier on page 114. Which are important to you long term and immediately? What do you need to do to make them happen? Many of them won't be critical, but you could incorporate them into your working life with a different slant. Would you benefit from a monthly session with a business coach or mentor? Do you need a loan from the bank to keep you watered, fed, sheltered and clothed?

Looking to leave the day job behind

You may be working in the day to get some money coming in and tackling your 'real' job at night, hoping to resign when you hit a breakthrough. If this sounds like you, make sure your 'night' job is honestly going places by asking the following questions:

* What have you achieved overall so far?
* What is working well?
* Where can you create more time in your day?
* Where do you want to be in six months' time?
* What will you need to do to make that happen?
* Who can help you further?
* What do you need to do to move your business to the next stage?
* How can you add value to your products and services so as to bring in extra income and enable you to focus more on the business and reduce the time you're spending on the day job?

Finally, keep your bank informed of how things are going. It's better to talk to them when problems are small rather than to wait until the day when they have grown out of all proportion. And be sure you are aware of all potential sources of help, support and expertise in the creative industries in your area.

Flexibility and adaptability go a long way to making the most of life

You may be merrily making your way through your career and then something happens which changes everything for you at a stroke.

Ten events which could change your life and your career

1   You meet your future partner; and life is never the same;
2   You create a baby and parenthood is on the way;
3   You hit on a business or social idea which, if implemented, will really make a difference;
4   You or one or your relatives or a friend falls seriously ill or has an accident and needs special care and love; plus it makes you re-think;
5   You get head-hunted;

6   A major world event makes you rethink life;
7   You volunteer for a cause you believe in;
8   You decide to live abroad;
9   You win the lottery;
10   You take the decision that you want to live a higher quality life
     and set about doing just that.

Keeping an interest in your degree

You've invested a number of years studying a subject at university,
and possibly before that, in order to gain the qualifications necessary to access your course. If you don't want to use the knowledge
you've acquired during your studies at work, you can still maintain
an interest in the subject. For example, you could:

1   Become a tutor at an adult education centre, or with WEA.
     You don't have to run a course for a year. There are many
     courses run solely for the day, which are designed to give peo-
     ple a taster or greater knowledge than they have already.
2   Tutor individuals who simply wish to better their knowledge.
3   Write about it, or set up a website.
4   Continue to work at it for your own enjoyment, practicing it
     in your own free time, going to shows and exhibitions for the
     fun of it.
5   Take courses at the local university where you are now, so that
     you keep your skills fresh – call up your local higher education
     institution to see what they have to offer.
6   Study something allied to what you did at university, to keep
     your brain active and alive and kicking.

Summary action points

Take responsibility for enhancing your own employability:

1   Keep a track of any ways in which recruitment methods for
     your sector change.
2   Who are the key players in the market you're in for recruit-
     ment? Who are the main agencies?
3   Don't stay with an employer if they're not enabling you to
     meet your career goals. Do what you can to ensure that the
     doors to your advancement are truly shut – and then leave.
     You could be surprised.

Chapter 10

Here's to life!

Take a holistic view of your life, and good health and happiness are more likely to be yours. Take a narrow, focused view of it, concentrating on only one aspect, and the others areas will suffer. There will be times one aspect of your life – such as your career – takes priority over others. But that doesn't mean that the rest of your life should lose out totally. If you're not fit and healthy for example, it will be harder to maintain a peak performance at work – which could make all the difference to whether you get that promotion or make that next step or not. Continually look at your life to consider questions such as:

- What do you want in your life besides your career?
- Who do you want in your life?
- What are you doing to enjoy life?
- What are you doing to pay off your loans?
- What are you doing to start building financial security for yourself?

We just have one life, so make time for those things which matter to you most, such as family, friends and fun. The way you manage your resources – time, energy, money, health and relationships – can make a huge difference to the quality of life you enjoy.

What are the things you want in your life to be happy and fulfilled? Do any of the examples in Table 10.1 below feature?

From the day we are born, life often gets in the way, throwing trials, tribulations and challenges at us. Working towards some 'wants' and 'must haves' in your life may demand that you 'park' other things aside for several weeks or months while you focus on them or a project that is of particular importance to you – such as your wedding day or training for a marathon. But a balance helps keep things

Table 10.1

Family – perhaps children	Key relationships and roles
Pets	Fun and laughter
Friends	Volunteering
Travel	Cultural and leisure activities
Dreams	Nature
Adventure	Excitement
Material goods	A good sex life
Achievements	Nice place to live
Financial assets	Solid retirement plans
Health and vitality	Great memories
Spirituality	Other

in perspective. And the work–life balance becomes a hot topic as individuals struggle to find ways to cope with the demands of work and personal commitments to family and friends. Balance is important in many aspects of life and Table 10.2 below gives suggestions as to where this balance is important.

How balanced is *your* life?

Every year, check your work–life balance is as you want. Assess how content you are with each area of your life which is important to you and to pinpoint those which need work and which you want to change.

Try this exercise to assess how well balanced your life is. For each of the categories you ticked in Table 10.1, consider the questions:

1   How satisfied are you right now with each one? Rate them individually from 0 to 10. Totally satisfied earns a 10; complete dissatisfaction at the centre a 0.
2   How does your life look? How many elements are a 10?

Table 10.2

Work	and	Leisure
Work	and	Holidays
Rest	and	Exercise
Healthy food	and	A bit of what you fancy
Smooth running of life	and	Challenges
Certainty	and	Uncertainty

3   Which ones need working on (i.e. are below a 7)? What would
    they have to be like for you to rank them as a 10?
4   What do you need to do to make that happen?
5   What will you do to make them happen and when?

You can keep doing this exercise over and over, enabling you to
make the changes you want in your life through a continual process
of making sure that every one is a 10, or at least working towards
it. In addition, you can repeat the exercise breaking down one element into various segments or units and grading each of them out
of 10. Health and fitness might be divided into areas such as fitness,
healthy eating, chill time, stretching and flexibility and smoking.

But work's taken over my life!

More employees are now finding that short breaks recharge their
batteries quite adequately without a huge panic about sorting out
the in-tray before and after a longer break. A good proportion put
off their holidays and don't take the full allowance, 'I'm too busy
at work'. Very few of us can keep going at premium performance
without having some sort of regular break built into the day. Our
own bodies have their own needs; one person may be able to do
with very little sleep, while others need a lot. If you don't listen to
your body, sooner or later it will pay you back when you least need
it, to remind you that it has needs too, such as proper rest and re-
cuperation. You're not indispensable. It's sad to say, but if you were
killed by a bus today, your company would go on without you. If
you don't look after yourself, you are unlikely to be able to look
after others.

There are some careers in which long hours are the norm, but it
can be easy to fall into the trap of doing long hours for the sake of
it. The person who never takes a lunch break can rarely work at the
same performance level throughout the day. The person who always
takes a break away from the phone, email and work environment
can only find her performance enhanced. No excuses! Walk around
the block for 20 minutes and boost your heart beat, reduce your
stress levels, keep that weight down and boost your mood.

Stress

With all the hype about stress, remember that the right sort of stress can help you live longer. Mild to moderate stress increases the production of brain cells, enabling them to function at peak capacity, so if you want to live life to a peak performance, get stressed but in the right way – it makes your body and mind stronger.

Beneficial stress gives you recovery time and a sense of accomplishment afterwards. It challenges you, although you may complain about it at the time. The bad stuff is prolonged, repeated, sustained and unrewarding. You need to find the middle ground somewhere between the two and build it into your daily life. Look for activities which reward and stimulate you, such as a run before work, studying in the evenings or voluntary work at weekends.

Get out of your comfort zone and take part in something which isn't routine and predictable or effortless. The more you look for these sorts of activities, the more you'll benefit. Collapsing in front of the TV after a day's work with a glass of wine isn't beneficial. Playing some sort of sport or going to adult education is. It's important to face stress or challenges mentally, physically, socially and spiritually. Don't waste time dwelling on the problems and demands of life – think about the pleasure, variety and vigour that challenges bring us and you'll feel much more alert and in control. Many challenges arrive through the roles we choose to play in life.

What roles do you want to play?

We all have roles in life and they all tend to appear at different times. Table 10.3 below shows roles most of us experience in our lives.

Our roles and relationships and the responsibilities that come with them intertwine with careers more than any other aspect of life. Which comes first: career or ageing relative? The presentation or a sick child? The school play or your squash game? The carer in us may play a key role and take centre stage in our lives while our parents get older and need decisions to be made for them. The parent has a lifelong role, but spends more time on it in the early years of a child's life and that role changes as life progresses, such that their children become their friends in adulthood. Our relationships with our siblings changes, too, particularly as we all settle down into adult life and face the challenges of dealing with ageing parents.

Table 10.3

Parent	Friend
Son/daughter	Volunteer
Manager	Leader
Supervisor	Confidante
Doer	Thinker
Teacher	Adviser
Loner	Niece/nephew
Aunt/uncle	Grandparent
Actor	Diplomat
Neighbour	Carer
Sister/brother	Cousin
Good Samaritan	Hero

Our friends, too, change. We keep some throughout life; others we see enter at different stages and then leave, as if they came for a reason. Perhaps they were there to teach us something, to make us laugh at a time when we felt low, to make us feel good about ourselves, or just … because. We need friends, both on our own account and when with a partner. Friends help you to keep things in perspective. A true friend is there for the good and bad times and will see you through.

If we're to have successful, empowering relationships, we need to put boundaries on what we will and won't do in our role. We may tire of the friend who calls us just once too often in the early hours of the morning, distraught over a break-up. We may be fed up of being the only sibling who makes an effort with our parents, while our siblings bleat that they are 'too busy'. Assertiveness is important if friendships and relationships are to thrive and grow. Saying 'no' is important in any role, if we are to feel strong and right. Saying 'yes' to keep the peace usually leads to feelings of resentment and disappointment in ourselves for not having the courage to say what we really want to say. Saying 'no' is a sign that we feel confident enough in ourselves to say what we mean and, crucially, that we care about ourselves and what we undertake in life.

The ability to manage yourself and others impacts on your ability to be personally effective in work and life. For example, if you have children, you will need to motivate them and get the family working as a team on projects to create a cohesive family unit. There will be times when you need to manage your own temper, when they do something which drives you to distraction for the hundredth time. Similarly, you will need to manage your client relationships at the office. If someone asks you for a piece of work which you know you cannot do within the timescale they give you, you will need to manage that and talk to them about it. You've learnt to manage people, situations and life at university and in your past life experience.

Develop your ability to handle people

1 Identify your boundaries in any relationship – the rules you feel comfortable with and stick to them.
2 Look at things from the other person's point of view. Put yourself in their shoes to get an idea for how they are feeling.
3 Remember that you cannot change other people – but you certainly can change the way you behave towards them.
4 Work on what you know you can influence, as opposed to the things you cannot.

Use your resources effectively

We have a tremendous amount of resources at our disposal, from mind-mapping to help creativity, speed reading to enable us to acquire knowledge more quickly, our memory to help retain it, meditation to help us focus and exercise to boost our energy. But the thing most people want more of today is time.

Is your time management letting you down?

'I haven't got time', is a common complaint. And yet how often do you reassess the way in which you spend your time (and money)?

♦ Track the ways in which you spend your time;
♦ Look back at your wheel of life and the activities you identified as important to you;
♦ How much of the 168 hours a week do you spend on them?
♦ Decide what to do about any imbalance;
♦ Track the way you spend your time for a week. In particular, track the time you're wasting on any of the activities in Table 10.4.

Table 10.4

Negative people/thoughts	Missing deadlines
Unanswered messages	Difficulty communicating
Outstanding letters and bills	Computer illiterate
Lacking confidence	Non-assertiveness
Unnecessary texting/emailing	Information overload
Losing things, e.g. keys	Smoking
Surfing the Internet	Drink and drugs
Broken items	Gambling
Too much TV	Fears
Poor sleep	Anxieties
Flitting from one thing to another without any real focus	Doubts
	Unnecessary meetings

Identify the three which waste most time for you and how much time they take up. What difference would it make if you didn't spend time on them? What are you going to do to get rid of them and what will you do with your time instead?

Undertake exercises like this while you're still at university, when you've graduated and later on when you have work, family and house maintenance responsibilities, when you are commuting and studying for professional qualifications, and have social and leisure activities to fit in. You can also apply it to your working day to find out how you can use your time more effectively at work.

Do the same exercise with money

- What financial base do you want to build up in the future?
- What do you need to do to make that happen?
- What is getting in the way?

Identify the financial resources you want and then you can start making them happen. Some items are essentials, such as a property to rent or buy, living costs and tax and state demands, e.g. national insurance. After that, saving is usually a wise move for that rainy day, and so is insurance. There are also a whole range of investments, savings accounts, stocks and shares which are best discussed with a financial adviser.

Ten ways to review your finances continually

1   Where is your money going?
2   Which items are essential, important, nice to have?

3 Where can you cut back?
4 What will you do to make that happen?
5 Which items do you no longer need and could sell?
6 How could you make more money? Examples include focusing on career development so that your salary increases.
7 Who can help you sort out your debts and finances?
8 What do banks and building societies offer graduates?
9 What realistically can you achieve in the next week, six months and three to five years? How can you capitalise on that? Put any unexpected windfalls such as a bonus or present into paying off your loan straight away.
10 How rigorously are you making your money work for you?

Make your money work for you. Be proactive in looking for the best deal, the highest interest rates which suit your needs, the lowest loan rates, and keep looking. Do a three-monthly financial MOT and reward yourself for your financial acumen. The higher you climb the career ladder, the greater the perks and salary. Working for professional qualifications at night will not only boost your employability but also keep you away from expensive bars and nightclubs, keep your money in your pocket and enable you to pay off your loans and debts faster.

Most people continually believe they are short of time and money, but don't proactively do enough specifically about it. It takes discipline, effort and creative thinking to sort out your finances. Paying off a loan doesn't take forever, even though it may seem like it. Much depends on how focused you are in paying off your loans. And if you nurture your career, your financial status should get better as you're rewarded for your efforts. Careers take up around 48 weeks a year out of 52 and subsequently impact on your overall quality of life, so surely they are worth the effort and dedication?

Living at home with your parents after university

Many young people are moving back home after university to save money, to pay off debts and for an assortment of other reasons. But what other options do you have apart from moving back in with your parent(s)? Could you get in touch with other graduates in the area or on the same graduate trainee scheme in your company who are in the same boat and flat-share, or live abroad in a country where graduates are welcomed and it is easier to get on the housing ladder? If you still decide to return home (perhaps you never left), work out a financial arrangement so that you pay your parent(s) rent (even if it is a very small amount) – you need to keep in the habit of budgeting for your housing. And arrange with them what your contribution will be towards the house-keeping, be it cleaning, washing, helping in the garden, cooking a meal a couple of times a week. Don't fall back into the ways of a teenager having everything done for you. You've moved on from that and so have your parents, so don't use your parents' home: sit up, take some responsibility and contribute to it. Sit down and agree a few house rules (just as you would have had at university with your flat mates) to keep everyone happy and remember to practice the art of negotiation and compromise. Finally, consider these questions:

- How long do you intend to stay with your parents? Give yourself a deadline to leave and stick to it. Do you want to be living with them when you're 40?
- How much of your student debt will you have paid off by that time? How will you do it?
- What will you have achieved in your career by then and how will that have boosted your income to help you start building a financial base?

Finally, when the time does come to move out, why not get your parents a small gift as a token of appreciation for their help over the years? Parents are usually very happy to help out their offspring – but it is always nice to be appreciated and thanked.

Don't forget the wild and wacky

What would your life be like if you drew up a list of all the things you wanted to do and achieved before your eightieth birthday? What a glorious blaze of memories you could have to look back on as your older years set in!

List the things you want to do and the reasons not to do them will fade into the background. You'll be filled with a tremendous energy and enthusiasm, passion and excitement as you start identifying how and when you're going to do it all. Writing your list down enhances your determination to make your items happen. Keep your list where you can easily see it frequently. Show your list to those who are important to you in your life. Suggest they draw up a list of their own, and compare notes. Are there things you can do together? Can you give each other the time and space required to make them happen? You need to make sure that those you love don't constrain you in a plant pot, so that your roots can't spread out and grow. If they do limit you, it may be time to say farewell to the relationship. A rich relationship should enable you to take some journeys as a couple and others alone.

Don't become a robot

It's easy to fall into a continuous cycle of work, supper, TV, bed. The more you do, the more you'll want to do and the dream list above can help you do just that! And as you push back your boundaries outside work, it will also become much easier to do just that in your working life. At the start of this book, you identified what success and happiness meant to you. Perhaps you listed things like a large bank account, exotic holidays, happy, healthy kids who stay off drugs and alcohol; giving something back to the community which really makes a difference, a particular status in the community or organisation.

You need to decide how important success is to you and in what capacity. Occasionally, you may tweak or transform your ideas of success and happiness or completely change them. But in the hustle, bustle and noise of life, take time out to dream and look into the present and future to ensure you're spending your life on activities which, and with people who, are important to you. Get focused and create the life and success you want.

Looking forward

The goal posts of life are for your own positioning. Be clear about the things you want to change in your life and what you want out of it, and then take personal responsibility to make it happen. You may need to work around barriers and obstacles, regulations and rules along the way, but that makes the end achievement all the more rewarding.

Your degree over, you have a chance to look back, contemplate, reflect and congratulate yourself, and to look forward, to plan and build your future. Pause to do this at regular intervals in your life and it will feature the activities and achievements which are important to you.

Finally, consider what really is important in life. Do any of these elements feature for you?

1   *Love* and be loved;
2   Be *passionate* about a cause;
3   *Wonder* at the beauty of the earth and nature's sheer power;
4   Feel at *peace*;
5   *Laugh* and see the funny side;
6   *Care* for those you know and those you don't;
7   Be *curious*: don't lose the habit of asking what, why, when, where, who, how;
8   *Learn* from those who've gone before you and who'll come after you;
9   Use your *creativity* and *imagination* to the full;
10 *Create* you own luck, success and happiness.

And remember:

Nobody ever said: 'I wish I'd spent more time at the office' on their deathbed.

Summary action points

Your life
Your future
Your choice
Good luck!

Further reading

Careers related

Alexander, L. (2003) *Turn Redundancy to Opportunity*, Oxford: How To Books Ltd.

Allworth Press: lots of books on arts and crafts at www.allworth.com.

Angell, R. (2004) *Getting into Films and Television*, Oxford: How To Books Ltd.

Britten, A. (2004) *Working in the Music Industry*, Oxford: How To Books Ltd.

Brown, C. (2005) *Working in the Voluntary Sector*, Oxford: How To Books Ltd.

Bruce, M. and Bessant, J. (2002) *Design in Business*, FT Prentice Hall.

Cox Review of Creativity in Business available at www.hm-treasury.gov.uk/cox

Gordon, B. (2003) *Opportunities in Commercial Art and Graphic Design Careers*, McGraw Hill Higher Education.

Heller, S. and Fernandes, T. (2005) *Becoming a Graphic Designer*, John Wiley & Sons Inc.

Kent, S. (2005) *Careers and Jobs in the Media*, London: Kogan Page Ltd.

Lees, J. (2005) *How to Get a Job You'll Love*, London: McGraw-Hill.

Williams, N. (2004), *The Work We Were Born to Do*, London: Element Books Ltd.

Further study

Marshall, S. and Green, N. (2004) *Your PhD Companion*, Oxford: How To Books Ltd. Contains a great selection of tips and advice to help you through your PhD.

Recruitment

Bishop-Firth, R. (2004) *CVs for High Flyers*, Oxford: How To Books Ltd.

Bryon, M. (2005) *Graduate Psychometric Test Workbook*, London: Kogan Page Ltd.

Johnstone, J. (2005) *Pass that Interview: Your Systematic Guide to Coming Out On Top*, Oxford: How To Books Ltd.

Yate, M.J. (2002) *The Ultimate CV Book*, London: Kogan Page Ltd.

Yate, M.J. (2003) *The Ultimate Job Search Letters Page*, London: Kogan Page Ltd.

Yate, M.J. (2005) *Great Answers to Tough Interview Questions*, London: Kogan Page Ltd.

Moving up the career ladder

Bishop-Firth, R. (2004) *The Ultimate CV for Managers and Professionals*, Oxford: How To Books Ltd.

Hughes, V. (2004) *Becoming a Director*, Oxford: How To Books Ltd.

Purkiss, J. and Edlmair, B. (2005) *How To Be Headhunted*, Oxford: How To Books Ltd.

Shavick, A. (2005) *Management Level Psychometric and Assessment Tests*, Oxford: How To Books Ltd.

Working abroad

Carte, P. and Fox, C. (2004) *Bridging the Culture Gap: A Practical Guide to International Business Communication*, London: Kogan Page Ltd.

Doing Business With, an excellent series published by Kogan Page Ltd covering these countries: Bahrain, Croatia, Saudi Arabia, UAE, China, Jordon, Kazakhstan, Kuwait, Lybia, Serbia and Montenegro and the EU Accession States.

Going to Live in … and *Living and Working in …* two highly informative and practical series published by How To Books Ltd (Oxford), covering countries such as Spain, Australia, New Zealand, France, Italy and Greece.

Khan-Panni, P. and Swallow, D. (2003) *Communicating Across Cultures*, Oxford: How To Books Ltd.

Reuvid, J. (2006) *Working Abroad: The Complete Guide to Overseas Employment*, London: Kogan Page Ltd.

Self-employment

Blackwell, E. (2004) *How to Prepare a Business Plan*, London: Kogan Page Ltd.

Bridge, R. (2004) *How I Made It: 40 Entrepreneurs Reveal All*, London: Kogan Page Ltd.

Gray, D. (2004) *Start and Run a Profitable Consultancy Business*, London: Kogan Page Ltd.

Isaacs, B. (2004) *Work For Yourself and Reap the Rewards*, Oxford: How To Books Ltd.

Jolly, A. (2005) *From Idea to Profit*, London: Kogan Page Ltd.

Power, P. (2005) *The Kitchen Table Entrepreneur*, Oxford: How To Books Ltd. Turn that hobby into a profitable business!

Reuvid, J. (2006) *Start Up and Run Your Own Business*, London: Kogan Page Ltd.

Whiteley, J. (2003) *Going for Self-Employment*, Oxford: How To Books Ltd.

Success

Drummond, N. (2005) *The Spirit of Success*, London: Hodder and Stoughton.

Ebury, S. (2003) *Moving On Up*, London: Ebury Press.

Hill, N. (1996) *Think and Grow Rich*, New York: Ballantine Books.

Robbins, A. (1991) *Awaken the Giant Within*, New York: Simon and Schuster.

Tracy, B. (2003) *Goals! How to Get Everything You Want – Faster Than You Ever Thought Possible*, San Francisco: Berrett-Koehler Publishers Inc.

Learning skills

Bradbury, A. (2006) *Successful Presentation Skills*, London: Kogan Page Ltd.

Claston, G. and Lucas, B. (2004) *Be Creative*, London: BBC Books Ltd.

Covey, S. (2005) *The 7 Habits of Highly Effective People: Powerful Lessons in Personal Change*, London: Simon & Schuster UK Ltd.

Lilley, R. (2006) *Dealing with Difficult People*, London, Kogan Page Ltd.

Quillam, S. (2003) *What Makes People Tick?* London: Element.

Wiseman, Dr R. (2004) *The Luck Factor: Change Your Luck – and Change Your Life*, Sydney: Random House Australia (Pty) Ltd.

Managing others

Charney, C. (2001) *Your Instant Adviser: The A–Z of Getting Ahead in the Workplace*, London: Kogan Page Ltd.

Morris, M.J. (2005) *The First-Time Manager*, London: Kogan Page Ltd.

Taylor, D. (2005) *The Naked Leader*, London: Bantam Books.

Whitmore, J. (2002) *Coaching for Performance*, London: Nicholas Brealey Publishing.

Building financial bases

Ahuja, A. (2004) *The Firt-Time Buyer's Guide*, Oxford: How To Books Ltd.

Bowley, G. (2005) *Making Your Own Will*, Oxford: How To Books Ltd.

Chesworth, N. (2004) *The Complete Guide to Buying and Renting Your First Home*, London: Kogan Page Ltd.

Palmer, T. (2005) *Getting Out of Debt and Staying Out*, Oxford: How To Books Ltd.

Life related

Fortgang, L.B. (2002) *Take Yourself to the Top*, London: Thorsons.

Gaskell, C. (2000) *Transform Your Life – 10 Steps to Real Results*, London: Thorsons.

Useful addresses and further information

UK general

Association of Graduate Careers Advisory Services
Administration Office
Millennium House
30 Junction Road
Sheffield S11 8XB
Tel: 0114 251 5750
www.agcas.org.uk

Hobsons
www.hobsons.com
A website with lots of features to help you get that right job worldwide

Prospects
www.prospects.ac.uk
A huge source of information and useful links for graduates of every discipline

UK regional graduate websites

Many of the sites below are designed to help graduates returning to the region or wishing to move to the area:

Yorkshire and Humber Region: www.graduatelink.com
Graduates Yorkshire: www.graduatesyorkshire.info
Graduates North East: www.graduates.northeast.ac.uk
Merseyside-Business Bridge www.business-bridge.org.uk
Merseyside: www.gieu.co.uk
Merseyside Workplace: www.merseyworkplace.com/

North West Student and Graduate On-Line: www.nwsago.co.uk
North Midlands and Cheshire Employers Directory: www.soc.
staffs.ac.uk/eh1/emp2003.html
Staffordshire Graduate Link: www.staffsgradlink.co.uk
Graduate Advantage – West Midlands: www.graduateadvantage.
co.uk
Gradsouthwest.com: www.gradsouthwest.com
GradsEast: www.gradseast.org.uk
The Careers Group, University of London: www.careers.lon.ac.uk
Graduate Ireland: www.gradireland.com
Scotland Graduate Careers, managed by Services to Graduates
Group: www.graduatecareers-scotland.org
Scotland – Graduates for Growth: www.graduatesforgrowth.co.uk
GO Wales: www.gowales.co.uk

Work experience, internships and voluntary work

Do It!
www.do-it.org
Find out what opportunities there are to volunteer in the region
you live in

GO Wales
www.gowales.co.uk

Graduate Business Partnership
run by the University of Exeter
www.ex.ac.uk/businessprojects

Knowledge Transfer Partnership
www.ktponline.org.uk/graduates

Merseyside-Business Bridge
www.business-bridge.org.uk
www.gieu.co.uk
Merseyside-related programme of events to enhance your employability and prepare you for a competitive job market with repre-
sentatives from various sectors

National Council for Work Experience
Tel: 0845 601 5510
www.work-expereince.org
enquiries@work-experience.org

West Midlands Graduate Advantage
www.graduateadvantage.co.uk

Further study

Association of MBAs
25 Hosier Lane
London EC1A 9LQ
Tel: 0207 246 2686
www.mbaworld.com
Has a full list of accredited MBA courses, plus links to institutions, and details of the MBA fair, scholarships, awards loans. The Official MBA Handbook can be acquired over their site and gives you all the information you need to get started. There's also information about rankings

British Council
10 Spring Gardens
London SW1A 2BN
Tel: 0161 957 7755
www.britcoun.org
The British Council has a network of offices throughout the UK and in 110 countries worldwide. Visit its website or one of its offices for more information on funding, scholarships and studying in the UK. You will also find a lot of information about Arts, Science and Society in the UK

National Union of Students
www.nusonline.org.uk

Ploteus
www.europa.eu.int/ploteus
The European course search portal

National Post-Graduate Committee
www.npc.org.uk
The NCP represents the interests of post-graduate students in the UK. Information on funding, discussion boards, post-graduate facts and issues, and post-graduate careers. Also an academic job search with international links to jobs in the USA, Canada and Australia among others

UKNARIC
Oriel House
Oriel Road
Cheltenham
Gloucestershire GL50 1XP
Tel: 0870 990 4088
www.naric.org.uk
The National Recognition Centre for the UK and National Agency for the Department for Education and Skills. The only official information provider on the comparability of international qualifications from over 180 countries

Post-graduate study and research

British Academy
www.britac.ac.uk

Find a Phd
www.FindAPhD.com
This website is the largest directory of PhD opportunities in the UK

Higher Education and Research Opportunities in the United Kingdom
www.hero.ac.uk
An excellent section on research with links to the main research councils, universities and others. Plus information on how to disclose your findings as a new researcher

Research Councils
www.research-councils.ac.uk
A partnership set up to promote science, engineering and technology supported by the eight UK Research Councils. Grants are allocated to individual researchers, networks of people working on projects, programmes, designated research centres, fellowships and postgraduate students

The Royal Society
www.royalsoc.ac.uk

The United Kingdom Research Office (UKRO)
www.ukro.ac.uk
An information and advice service on research and higher education

Universities UK
www.universitiesuk.ac.uk

Self-employment

British Franchise Association
Thames View
Newton Road
Henley-on-Thames
Oxon RH9 1HG
Tel: 01491 578 050
www.thebfa.org
For information on franchises, both in and outside the UK, finding
a franchise, successful case studies and events, a list of members.
Check when the next Franchise Exhibition is near you on its web-
site and there's also information on international franchises.

BusinessLink
www.businesslink.gov.uk
A network of business advice centres in England with allied bodies
in Scotland, Wales and Northern Ireland, all accessible through this
site

www.docrafts.co.uk
A resource with information on projects, events, stocklists, top tips
and the ability to use the site to track your own events, projects,
etc. Plus you can craft chat

Prime Initiative
Astral House
1268 London Road
London SW16 4ER
Tel: 0208 765 7833
www.primeinitiative.org.uk/
Dedicated to helping those over 50 to set up their own business

Prince's Trust
Tel: 0800 842 842
www.princes-trust.org.uk
Help for the 14–30 year old who wants to set up his or her own
business or tackle barriers to employment

Shell LiveWIRE
www.shell-livewire.org/
Unlock your potential with this excellent site. Plus financial action planning and a fabulous business encyclopaedia. For 16–30 year olds who want to start and develop their own business

Start-ups
www.startups.co.uk

Life drawing models
www.modelreg.com
The UK site and professional organisation for life models, dedicated to life art – a membership list known as the Red List of models available on licence to tutors, artists, colleges, photographers and art groups. Revised and sent out four times a year. Over 400 models are listed, with contact details, location and rough times available

Job sites

Animated People
www.animatedpeople.com
Examples of vacancies in the games industry from a major employer

www.artsjobsonline.com
Advertising arts jobs in the UK and Ireland, a relatively new site and blissfully simple to use, for job seekers or employers

Careers in Design
www.careersindesign.co.uk
Offers help to graduates

Eden Brown Recruitment agency
www.edenbrown.com

Get a Life
www.getalife.org.uk
Careers guidance and information for the public sector

The Guardian
www.media.guardian.co.uk/newmedia
Provides the latest news and links to recruitment sites with a huge jobs section

The Knowledge
www.theknowledgeonline.com
Database of useful contacts in film, TV and video production

www.mad.co.uk
This online magazine of the art and design trade publications
encompasses Marketing Week, Instore Marketing and Design Week

Media Circle
www.mediacircle.co.uk
For you if you want to work in media sales selling to advertisers

Mediamoves
www.workinublishing.org.uk
Jobs in the publishing industry

National Campaign for the Art
www.artscampaign.org.uk
Vacancies in arts marketing, administration, development and the
media

Spotlight
www.spotlightcd.com
Publishes casting directories in constant use by film, TV and theat-
rical companies

The Stage
www.thestage.co.uk
For people who want to get into the industry but also pulls
together those already working in it with vacancies, mostly of a
technical nature but also general arts

Universities, colleges and schools

www.jobs.ac.uk
The official recruitment website for staffing in higher education

www.jobs.tes.co.uk
The *Times Educational Supplement* with lots of vacancies in
education

Professional organisations and trade associations

The following are examples of professional and trade associations which relate to business and finance. Many have international links with their peers abroad, so research their websites thoroughly.

International organisations

International Federation of Interior Architects/Interior Designers
www.ifiworld.org

International Council of Societies of Industrial Design
ICSID Secretariat
455 St Antoine W., Suite S510
Montreal
Quebec H2Z LJ1
Canada
Tel: +1 514 448 4949
www.icsid.org
Employment and internship opportunities, with CV and portfolio posting for employers searching for new staff

International Council of Graphic Design Associations
ICOGRADA Secretariat
455 St Antoine W., Suite S510
Montreal
Quebec H2Z 1J1
Canada
Tel: +1 514 448 4949
www.icograda.org
secretariat@icograda.org

Creative Clusters
www.creativeclusters.com
An international conference and network for people working in the development of the creative industries

AIGA
www.aiga.org
The USA professional organisation for design

Interior-Design
www.interior-design.us
Interior design in the USA

Sugarloaf Craft Festivals in the USA
www.sugarloafcrafts.com
Designer arts and craft shows

Society of Creative Designers
www.craftdesigners.org
For craft designers in the USA

The Designers Institute of New Zealand
www.dinz.org.nz

New Zealand Trade and Enterprise
www.nzte.govt.nz

Culture Base
www.culturebase.net/mission.php
A database an international source on international artists, performers and promoters

Visiting Arts
Bloomsbury House
74–77 Great Russell Street
London WC1B 3DA
Tel: 0207 291 1600
www.visitingarts.org.uk
For visiting artists to the UK

UK Based

Creative and Cultural Skills
11 Southwark Street
London SE1 1RQ
Tel: 0207 089 5866
www.ccskills.org.uk

Royal Society of Arts
8 John Adam Street
London WC2N 6EZ
Tel: 0207 930 5115

Advertising

Advertising Association
7th Floor North
Artillery House
11–19 Artillery Row
London SW1P 1RT
Tel: 0207 340 1100
www.adassoc.org.uk
aa@adassoc.org.uk
You can download the AA's careers guide *Getting Into Advertising* from its website

Advertising Producers Alliance
47 Beak Street
London W1F 9SE
Tel: 0207 434 2651
www.a-p-a.net
info@a-p-a.net

CAM Foundation Ltd
(Communications and Marketing Education Foundation Ltd)
Moor Hall
Cookham
Maidenhead
Berks SL6 9QH
Tel: 01628 427 120
www.camfoundation.com
info@camfoundation.com

European Association of Communication Agencies
EACA Secretariat
152 Blvd. Brand Whitlock
B-1200 Bruxelles
Tel: (32-2) 740 07 10
www.eaca.be

Institute of Practitioners in Advertising
44 Belgrave Square
London SW1X 8QS
Tel: 0207 235 7020
www.ipa.co.uk

Architecture

Architectural Registration Board
8 Weymouth Street
London W1N 5BU
Tel: 0207 580 5861
www.arb.org.uk

Royal Institute of British Architects
66 Portland Place
London W1B 1AD
Tel: 0207 580 5533
www.riba.org

Arts

Arts Advice
Tel: 0800 093 0444
www.artsadvice.com

Arts Council England
14 Great Peter Street
London SW1P 3NQ
Tel: 0845 300 6200
www.artscouncil.org.uk

Arts Council of Wales
Museum Place
Cardiff CF10 3NX
Tel: 029 2037 6500
www.artswales.org.uk

Arts Marketing Association
7a Clifton Court
Clifton Road
Cambridge CB1 7BN
Tel: 01223 578078
www.a-m-a.co.uk
info@a-m-a.co.uk

Northern Ireland Arts Council
77 Malone Road
Belfast BT9 6AQ
Tel: 028 9038 5200
www.artscouncil-ni.org

Scottish Arts Council
12 Manor Place
Edinburgh EH3 7DD
Tel: 0131 226 6051
www.sac.org.uk

Ceramics

Association for Ceramic Training and Development
St James House
Webberley Lane
Longton
Stoke-on-Trent ST3 1RJ
Tel: 01782 597016
www.actd.co.uk

Colourists

Society of Dyers and Colourists
PO Box 244
Perkin House
82 Grattan Road
Bradford
West Yorkshire BD1 2JB
Tel: 01274 725 138
www.sdc.org.uk
education@sdc.org.uk

Computing

British Computer Society
1st Floor, Block D
North Star House
North Star Avenue
Swindon
Wiltshire SN2 1FA
Tel: 0845 300 4417
www.bcs.org.uk

Entertainment Leisure Software Publishers Association
www.elspa.com

UK Web Design Association
Fareham Enterprise Centre
Hackett Way
Fareham
Hampshire PO14 1TH
www.ukwda.org

Clothing

Clothing and Allied Products Industry Training Board (CAPITB)
80 Richardshaw Lane
Pudsey
Leeds
West Yorkshire LS28 6BN
Tel: 0113 239 3355
www.careers-in-clothing.co.uk
capitbtrust@capitbtrust.org.uk

British Hat Guild
PO Box 48664
London NW8 6WS
Tel: 01582 481821
www.britishhatguild.co.uk
info@britishhatguild.co.uk

Crafts

Crafts Council
44a Pentonville Road
London N1 9BY
Tel: 0207 278 7700
www.craftscouncil.org.uk

Craft Potters' Association
25 Foubert's Place
London W1F 7QF
Tel: 0207 437 6781

Design

Chartered Society of Designers
1 Cedar Court
Royal Oak Yard
Bermondsey Street
London SE1 3GA
Tel: 0207 357 8008
www.csd.org.uk

Design Council
34 Bow Street
London WC2E 7DL
Tel: 0207 420 5200
www.design-council.org.uk
www.yourcreativefuture.org
info@design-council.org.uk

National Society for Education in Art and Design (NSEAD)
The Gatehouse
Corsham Court
Wiltshire SN13 OBZ
Tel: 01249 714 825
www.nsead.org

The following sites may also be useful:

www.britishdesign.co.uk: British Design Innovation
www.bedg.org: British European Design Group
www.creativexport.co.uk: Creative Export
www.cfsd.org.uk: Centre for Sustainable Design
www.dandad.co.uk: D&AD, an educational charity which gives
funds and awards and promotes young designers and education
www.dba.org.uk: Design Business Association
www.designinbusiness.org.uk: Design in Business
wwwdesignmuseum.org: Design Museum
www.designresearchsociety.org: Design Research Society
www.dffn.org: Design for Future Needs
www.hhrc.rca.ac.uk: Helen Hamlyn Research Centre
www.interiordesignhandbook.com: Interior Design Handbook
www.designinparliament.org.uk: Associated Parliamentary Group
for Design and Innovation
www.webdesignforbusiness.com: Design for Business

Fashion

UK Fashion Exports
www.ukfashionexports.com

Fashion Career Centre
www.fashioncareercenter.com
A USA site

Fashion Group International
www.fgi.org
A global non-profit association with over 6,000 professionals representing the fashion and allied industries

www.stylecareer.com/
Lots of tips and practical advice on breaking into the fashion and image industry (USA)

Illustrators

Association of Illustrators
2nd Floor, Back Building
150 Curtain Road
London EC2A 3AR
Tel: 0207 613 4328
www.theAOI.com

The Society of Illustrators (USA)
www.societyillustrators.org

Interior Décor

Furniture, Funishings and Interiors National Training Organisation
67 Wollaton Road
Beeston
Nottingham NG9 2NG
Tel: 0115 922 1200
www.ffinto.org

Jewellers

British Jewellers Association
10 Vyse Street
Birmingham B18 6LT
www.bja.org.uk

Gemmological Association and Gem Testing Laboratory of Great Britain
27 Greville Street
London EC1N 8TN
Tel: 0207 404 3334
www.gagtl.ac.uk
information@gem-a.info

National Association of Goldsmiths
78a Luke Street
London EC2A 4XG
Tel: 0207 613 4445
www.jewellers-online.org

The Goldsmiths' Company
Goldsmiths' Hall
Foster Lane
London EC2V 6BN
Tel: 0207 606 7010
www.thegoldsmiths.co.uk

Multimedia

British Interactive Multimedia Association
Briarlea House
Southend Road
Billericay CM11 2PR
Tel: 01277 658107
www.bima.co.uk

Newspapers/Journalism

National Union of Journalists
Headland House
308–312 Gray's Inn Road
London WC1X 8DP
Tel: 0207 278 7916
www.nujtraining.org.uk

National Council for the Training of Journalists
Latton Bush Centre
Southern Way
Harlow
Essex CM18 7BL
Tel: 01279 430 009
www.nctj.com

Newspaper Society
74–77 Great Russell Street
London WC1B 3DA
Tel: 0207 636 7014
www.newspapersoc.org.uk

Photography

Association of Photographers
81 Leonard Street
London EC2A 4QS
Tel: 0207 739 6669
www.the-aop.org
general@aophoto.co.uk

British Institute of Professional Photography
Fox Talbot House
2 Amwell End
Ware
Herts SG12 9HN
Tel: 01920 464 011
www.bipp.com

Printing

Institute of Paper, Printing and Publishing
83 Guildford Street
Chertsey
Surrey KT16 9AS
Tel: 0870 330 8625
www.ip3.org.uk

Scottish Print Employers Federation
48 Palmerston Place
Edinburgh EH12 5DE
Tel: 0131 220 4353
www.spef.org.uk

Television and film

BECTU (independent union for those working in broadcasting)
373–377 Clapham Road
London SW9 9BT
Tel: 0207 346 0900
www.bectu.org.uk
info@bectu.org.uk

BBC Recruitment Services
PO Box 48305
London W12 6YE
www.bbc.co.uk/jobs

British Kinematograph Sound and Television Society
The Moving Image Society
Pinewood Studios
Iver Heath
Bucks SL0 0NH
Tel: 01753 656 656
www.bksts.com

CFP Europe
Bernhard Bangs Allé 25
2000 Frederiksberg
Denmark
Tel: +45 33 86 28 91
www.cfp-e.com
cfp-e@cfp-e.com

Five
22 Long Acre
London WC2E 9LY
www.five.tv
www.five.tv/aboutfive/recruitment/

British Film Institute
www.bfi.org.uk

ITV Network Ltd
200 Gray's Inn Road
London EC1X 8HF
www.itv.com

Skills for Media (New Media Careers Information service from Skillset and BECTU)
Skillset, The Sector Skills Council or the Audio Visual Industries
Prospect House
80–110 New Oxford Street
London WC1A 1HB
Tel: 08080 300 900
www.skillsformedia.com
info@skillset.org

Textiles

American Apparel and Footwear Association
www.apparelandfootwear.org

Register of Apparel and Textiles Designers
5 Portland Place
London W1B 1PW
Tel: 0207 636 5577
www.ukfashionexports.com

Textile Institute
www.texi.org

Theatre

Association of British Theatre Technicians
55 Farringdon Road
London EC1 3JB
Tel: 0207 242 9200
www.abtt.org.uk

Society of British Theatre Designers
Fourth Floor
55 Farringdon Road
London EC1M 3JB
Tel: 0207 242 9200
www.theatredesign.org.uk

eBooks – at www.eBookstore.tandf.co.uk

A library at your fingertips!

eBooks are electronic versions of printed books. You can store them on your PC/laptop or browse them online.

They have advantages for anyone needing rapid access to a wide variety of published, copyright information.

eBooks can help your research by enabling you to bookmark chapters, annotate text and use instant searches to find specific words or phrases. Several eBook files would fit on even a small laptop or PDA.

NEW: Save money by eSubscribing: cheap, online access to any eBook for as long as you need it.

Annual subscription packages

We now offer special low-cost bulk subscriptions to packages of eBooks in certain subject areas. These are available to libraries or to individuals.

For more information please contact webmaster.ebooks@tandf.co.uk

We're continually developing the eBook concept, so keep up to date by visiting the website.

www.eBookstore.tandf.co.uk